HELLO! USA

Everyday Living for International Residents and Visitors

---

by Judy Priven
©Hello! America, Inc. 1996

Acknowledgments

Author: Judy Priven

Editors: Sarah Cogan, the Grammarians; David Thurston

Associate editors: Kathleen Ebel, Lynn Ulivieri, Ana Valenzuela

Artwork and cover design: Wendy Weidemann, Weidemann & Associates

Page design and desktop publishing: Alma Lopez, Creative Communicators, LLC

Special thanks to Sylvia Porter, Community Liaison Officer, Embassy of Australia

---

Published by:
Hello! America, Inc.

Distributed by:
Conquest Corporation
P.O. Box 250488
Franklin, MI 48025
800/922-6629
810/355-4910

ISBN 0-9635633-2-7

Hello! USA: Everyday Living for International Residents and Visitors

How to Use
__Hello!™USA__

First Pages

In an Emergency: what to do and say.   **Staying Safe:** basic rules for staying safe.

Chapters*

Chapter openers: maps; pictures of everyday objects & forms, sample conversations
Chapter text: American customs and ways of doing things.

1,2,3... step-by-step directions
(what you should do first, second...and last)

"Words to Know": American words used in everyday life.

 documents or papers you need

 time to start

 warning
(what *not* to do; what to watch out for)

 cost**

 answers to questions you might ask

Appendix

"Chapter Information": telephone numbers and addresses.
"Help!": simple rules for avoiding crime and getting help in an emergency

*   The Publisher is not responsible for any information or advice given by the stores and services listed here.
** The costs on these pages are good for the spring of 1996. Many of these costs may be higher in a short time.
Other costs are estimates; they are not exact. Be sure to find out for yourself how much to pay.

Content Advisors

These persons contributed directly to the development and review of *Hello! USA*. The author is grateful to each of them for giving so generously of his or her time and expertise.

Arrival and "Settling In" Services

Peggy Lovett, President
Full Circle Relocation
7918 Jones Branch Rd. Suite 230
McLean, VA 22102
Tel: 703/448-1902; Fax: 703/448-8674

Jane R. Smith, President
Linda Birtwhistle, Coordinator of
International Programs
Options Resource &
Career Center, Inc.
1200 Blalock, Suite 109
Houston, TX 77055
Tel: 713/465-1118; Fax: 713/465-9249
OptionsHou@aol.com

International and Domestic Moves

Bill Musser,
International Marketing Representative
United Van Lines
1 United Drive
Fenton, MO 63026
Tel: 314/349-2883;
    1-800/325-3924;
Fax: 314/326-0307

Appliance Preparation

Allen Sausen, President
Appliances Overseas, Inc.
276 Fifth Ave. Suite 407
New York, NY 10001
Tel: 212/545-8001; Fax: 212/545-8005
E-mail: applover@village.ios.com

Immigration Issues

Elizabeth Espin-Stern, Esq.
Shaw, Pittman, Potts, & Trowbridge
2300 N St.
Washington, DC 20037
Tel: 202/663-8515; Fax: 202/663-8007

American Customs and Behaviors

Jane Adams, Field Staff Consultant
The World Bank
Washington, DC

220-Volt Electronics

James Evanoff, Marketing Director
Keno Electronics
International Mall
1401 University Blvd.
Hyattsville, MD 20783
Tel.: 1-800/422-5366
      301/431-1366;
Fax: 301/445-0610

Banking, Credit Cards, & Loans

Michèle Imhoff
France Ponsart
Banque Transatlantique
U.S. Representative Office
1819 H St., NW #620
Washington, DC 20006
Tel: 202/429-1909; Fax: 202/296-7294

U.S. Taxes

M.J. Kittell
KPMG Peat Marwick LLP
1600 Market St.
Philadelphia, PA 19103
Tel: 215/299-3906; Fax: 215/299-1475

Insurance

James J. Krampen, President
Specialty Risk International, Inc.
9449 Priority Way West Drive,
Suite 150
Indianapolis, IN 46240
Tel: 800/335-0611
    317-575-2652; Fax:317/575-2659

English Instruction

Deidre Doyle, Deputy Director
inlingua School of Languages
1901 N. Moore St., MS-02
Arlington, VA 22209
Tel: 800/293-5214
    703/527-8666; Fax: 703/527-8693

Colleges & Universities

Deidra Razzaque,
Student Services Administrator
Foreign Student Service Council
2337 18th St. NW
Washington, DC 20009
Tel: 202/232-4979; Fax: 202/667-9305

Cheryl Finkelstein
Dean of Enrollment Management and
Student Development
North Shore Community College
1 Ferncroft Rd.
Danvers, MA 01923-0840
Tel: 508/762-4000

Maria Leviste
Assistant Director
Florida International University
International Student
& Scholar Services
University Park, Miami, FL 33199
Tel: 305/348-2421; Fax: 305/348-1521

Table of Contents

Introduction: Our Country: Its States & Cities

Coming and Going

Fun and Friends

When You Get Here

Settling In

Your Children

Higher Education

Index

__Our Country__
Its States & Cities

Northeast

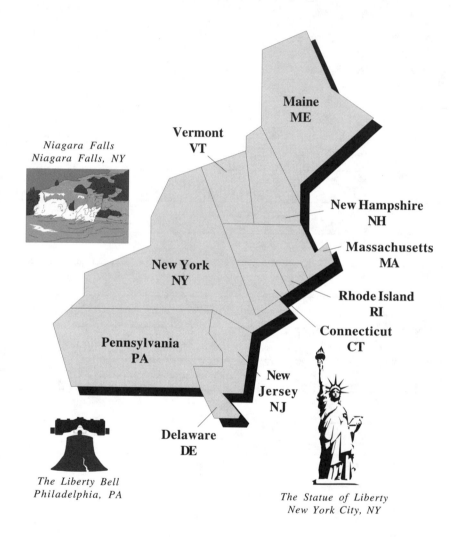

Niagara Falls
Niagara Falls, NY

Maine
ME

Vermont
VT

New Hampshire
NH

Massachusetts
MA

New York
NY

Rhode Island
RI

Connecticut
CT

Pennsylvania
PA

New
Jersey
NJ

Delaware
DE

The Liberty Bell
Philadelphia, PA

The Statue of Liberty
New York City, NY

Author's Favorites

Foods I love

 *Maine lobster.* Served boiled, broiled, steamed, or stuffed. Found all along the New England coast.

New England clam chowder. Thick and creamy soup. Different from Manhattan clam chowder, which has a tomato base.

Good times I've had

*Buggy-riding through Pennsylvania Dutch Country. Lancaster, PA (717/394-6185) A trip into a different world, with Amish farmhouses and country roads.

"Dressing up" to see an opera at the elegant Metropolitan Opera House, Lincoln Center. New York City, NY (212/362-6000)

Driving through the tree-lined streets in the fall. Anywhere in the Northeast. The leaves are bright gold and red.

Riding into the Falls. Niagara Falls, New York (716/278-1701). You feel the spray as the boat goes right up to the Falls.

Strolling through Harvard Yard and other college campuses. Boston, MA (617/495-1573 or 800/447-6277.) Also, strolling down the Freedom Trail, a 2½-mile walk through American-Revolution sites.

Whitewater rafting. New England Outdoor Center. Kennebec River, ME (1-800-766-7238) A thrilling ride on fast-moving river waters. You can also hike, canoe, and cross-country ski at the Outdoor Center.

*Especially for children

South

The White House

Our Nation's Capital
Washington DC

The Kentucky Derby
Lexington, KY

Derby Days

West Virginia
WV

Maryland
MD

North
Carolina
NC

Virginia
VA

Kentucky
KY

Tennessee
TN

Oklahoma
OK

Arkansas
AR

Georgia
GA

South
Carolina
SC

Texas
TX

Louisiana
LA

Alabama
AL

Mississippi
MS

Florida
FL

★★★★★
RODEO

The Kennedy Space Center
near Orlando, FL

Author's Favorites

Foods I love

Crabs, boiled and spiced. Served in the shell, which you break open with a hammer. Maryland crabs are best. Also, softshell crabs in season, when the crab has shed its hard shell has not yet grown a new one.

Southern fried chicken. Chicken dipped in a thick batter and deep-fried. Most popular all through the Southeast.

 Texas beef. Any way you like it—steaks, hamburgers, or pot roast. BBQ (barbecued) ribs are my favorite—grilled outdoors with a spicy tomato sauce.

Good times I've had

Climbing into the Apollo 11 space module. National Air & Space Museum, Washington DC (202/357-2700). Also, the other nine Smithsonian museums and galleries, the White House and the Capitol—all free.

*Listening to Rock and Roll. Graceland, Memphis, TN (901/332-3322) The estate of Elvis Presley, the famous rock and roll singer.

Nightclubbing. The French Quarter, New Orleans, LA (504/566-5046). A historic area with jazz clubs, Creole restaurants, art galleries. The first Creoles were French settlers.

*Riding down the Texas Cyclone. Astroworld and Waterworld, Houston, TX (713-799-1234. A huge amusement park, with about 100 rides. Don't go on the Cyclone unless you like to be scared! Also, you can take a tram ride through NASA's Johnson Space Center (713/244-2100).

*Shaking hands with Donald Duck and other Disney characters. Disney World, Orlando, FL (407/824-4321)

* Sipping free samples of Coca-Cola. The World of Coca-Cola, Atlanta, GA (404/676-5151) A 3-story museum about the history of this famous drink.

Teeing off. The Pinehurst Resort, Pinehurst Village, NC (910/295-8141) One of the top-rated golf courses in the country.

*Watching the racing horses. Kentucky Horse Park, Lexington, KY (606/233-4303). Home of the famous Kentucky Derby. Horse shows, horse farm tours, and films on past races.

*Especially for children

Midwest

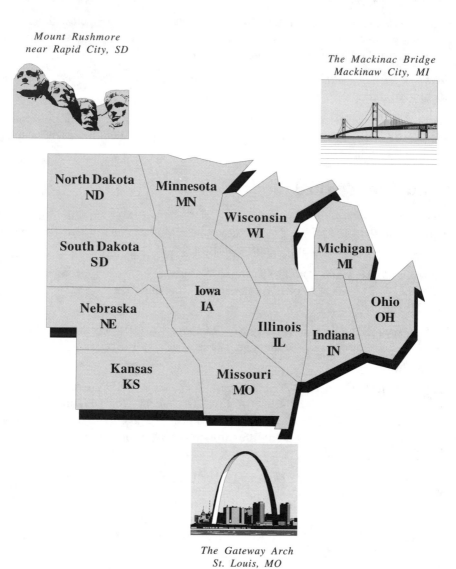

*Mount Rushmore
near Rapid City, SD*

*The Mackinac Bridge
Mackinaw City, MI*

**North Dakota
ND**

**Minnesota
MN**

**Wisconsin
WI**

**South Dakota
SD**

**Michigan
MI**

**Iowa
IA**

**Nebraska
NE**

**Illinois
IL**

**Ohio
OH**

**Indiana
IN**

**Kansas
KS**

**Missouri
MO**

*The Gateway Arch
St. Louis, MO*

Author's Favorites

Foods I Love

Macaroni & cheese. Best when baked with extra-sharp cheddar cheese from Wisconsin.

 Corn on the cob. Wrapped in tin foil and baked over the grille at a barbecue. Served with salt and butter over the corn; you pick up the cob with your hands and bite off the corn. The states of Illinois, Indiana, Iowa, and Ohio are known as "The Cornbelt."

Cherry pie. More than four million cherry trees grow around Lake Michigan. People from the Midwest also put them in soups, jams, and meat sauces.

Good times I've had

*Bicycling along the water. Mackinac Island, Mackinaw City, MI (906/847-7383) Views of the bridge and ships. Also, horse-drawn tours to historic sites from the American Revolution and the War of 1812.

*Dancing the "frug." The Henry Ford Museum & Greenfield Village, Dearborn, MI (1-800/TELL-A-FRIEND). Exhibit of popular music from the '60s–'70s. Walk through the real rooms of famous Americans—such as Henry Ford and Abraham Lincoln. Also, an exhibit of antique cars such as the "Model T" Ford.

Looking at Seurat's Sunday Afternoon on the Island of La Grande Jatte. The Art Institute of Chicago, Chicago, IL (312/443-3600) Western Art collection, exhibits of home decorations, and a re-creation of an old Stock Exchange Trading Room. Also in Chicago—Second City, one of the best comedy clubs in the U.S.

Photographing the busts of the presidents with the lights at night. Mt. Rushmore National Memorial, Keystone, SD (605/574-2523) The busts of Presidents Washington, Jefferson, Lincoln, and Roosevelt (Theodore) carved in a granite cliff.

*Shopping. Mall of America, Bloomington, MN (612/883-8800) The largest indoor mall in the world, with more than 400 stores and an amusement park.

*Especially for children

West

**Alaska
AK**

*Old Faithful
Yellowstone National Park, WY*

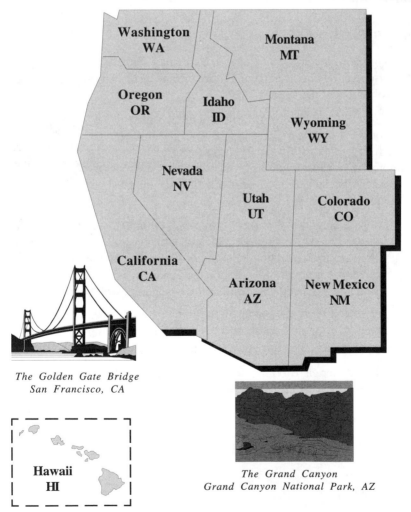

**Washington
WA**

**Montana
MT**

**Oregon
OR**

**Idaho
ID**

**Wyoming
WY**

**Nevada
NV**

**Utah
UT**

**Colorado
CO**

**California
CA**

**Arizona
AZ**

**New Mexico
NM**

*The Golden Gate Bridge
San Francisco, CA*

**Hawaii
HI**

*The Grand Canyon
Grand Canyon National Park, AZ*

Author's Favorites

Foods I love

Chili. Beans, tomato, and spices—especially chili powder. A thick "soup" made either "con carne" with meat or vegetarian. Usually served with cheese on top.

Baked potatoes. Idaho baking potatoes are best.

Salmon. A red or pink fish most easily caught in fresh water. Best when broiled or baked. Smoked salmon, or lox, is also popular, but very expensive. You can buy salmon fresh from the stalls at Pike Place Market in Seattle.

Good times I've had

Photographing moose and bear. Denali National Park, AK (907/683-2294 or 907/683-1266) Also, Flying above the mountains (weather permitting), fishing, hiking, and camping.

Riding a mule down the Grand Canyon. Grand Canyon National Park, AZ (520/638-7888) ½-day, full-day, or 2-day trips. Short rides for children.

Shopping for Native American (Indian) art at the pueblos near Santa Fe, NM (505/983-7317) Also, taking a tour of the pueblo to see how Native Americans live today.

Sipping champagne in a hot-air balloon. Napa, CA (707/253-2222 or 707/944-0288) A "fun" way to see the Wine Country just north of San Francisco.

Skiing, downhill. Vail, CO (970/476-5677) Probably the highest-rated ski area in the country; the Vail resort alone has 4,014 acres of runs, a gondola, 24 lifts, and a 3,250-foot drop. Also, cross-country skiing, ice skating, snowmobiling nearby, with golf in the warmer months (970/476-5601)

Watching the song-and-dance shows at the big hotels. Las Vegas, NV (702/735-1616) Bally's or Caesar's Palace are best.

*Especially for children

Cities & Climates

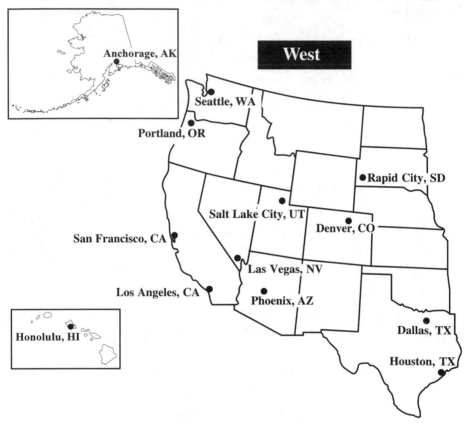

City	Average Temps		Sunny Days
	Lowest **F° / C°**	**Highest** **F° / C°**	**Average # per year**
Anchorage, AK	6 / -14	65 / 18	61
Dallas, TX	34 / 1	98 / 37	137
Denver, CO	16 / -9	88 / 31	115
Honolulu, HI	65 / 18	87 / 31	88
Houston, TX	41 / 5	94 / 34	95
Las Vegas, NV	33 / 1	104 / 40	211
Los Angeles, CA	48 / 9	84 / 29	186
Phoenix, AZ	39 / 4	105 / 41	212
Portland, OR	34 / 1	80 / 27	68
Rapid City, SD	9 / -13	87 / 31	111
Salt Lake City, UT	20 / -7	93 / 34	125
San Franciso, CA	44 / 7	69 / 21	167
Seattle, WA	34 / 1	75 / 24	57

Cities & Climates

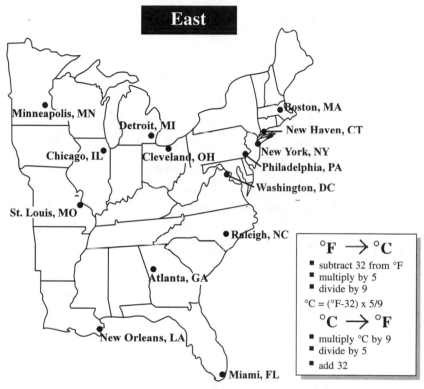

East

°F → °C
- subtract 32 from °F
- multiply by 5
- divide by 9

°C = (°F-32) x 5/9

°C → °F
- multiply °C by 9
- divide by 5
- add 32

City	Average Temps		Sunny Days
	Lowest F°/C°	**Highest** F°/C°	**Average # per year**
Atlanta, GA	33 / 1	89 / 32	110
Boston, MA	23 / -5	82 / 28	99
Chicago, IL	14 / -10	83 / 28	133
Cleveland, OH	19 / -7	82 / 28	70
Detroit, MI	16 / -9	83 / 28	77
Miami, FL	59 / 15	89 / 32	77
Minneapolis, MN	2 / -17	83 / 28	97
New Haven, CT	23 / -5	82 / 28	100
New Orleans, LA	43 / 6	91 / 33	103
New York, NY	26 / -3	85 / 29	107
Philadelphia, PA	24 / -4	86 / 30	93
Raleigh, NC	29 / -2	88 / 31	112
St. Louis, MO	20 / -7	90 / 32	103
Washington, DC	28 / -2	89 / 32	98

11

⬛ From ⬛ City to City

WEST

	Denver	Houston	Los Angeles	Phoenix	Seattle	
Dallas	799	242	1385	1015	2093	miles
Dallas	1286	389	2228	1634	3371	kilometers
Las Vegas	756	1484	265	292	1204	miles
Las Vegas	1216	2388	426	470	1938	kilometers

EAST

	Atlanta	Boston	New Orleans	St. Louis	Washington, DC	
Chicago	678	986	934	287	688	miles
Chicago	1091	1586	1503	462	1107	kilometers
Miami	665	1510	867	1222	1074	miles
Miami	1070	2430	1395	1966	1728	kilometers

From Coast to Coast

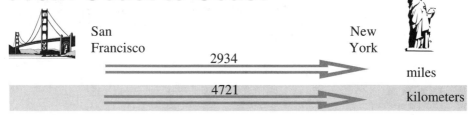

San Francisco → New York

2934 miles

4721 kilometers

1 mile = 1.6 kilometers

1 kilometer = .6 miles

Note: These are the distances for driving the fastest way from city to city.

Coming and Going

Before You Come

Money

Cash in U.S. dollars

Traveler's checks in U.S. dollars

Credit cards

Documents

Entry papers

Financial history/ bank routing information

Medical history/ medicine prescriptions

Birth certificate

Driving history and auto information

Education records and diplomas

What to Find Out

Legal status

If you are coming to the U.S. for the first time, you may be wondering:

- How long can I stay?
- Who can come with me?
- How often can I travel outside the U.S.?
- Will my husband or wife be able to work?

The answers to these questions are different for every person or family (see chapter on "Your Legal Status"); even if you have been here before, these answers may have changed. If possible, contact an immigration attorney before you leave; make sure you:

- have the type of visa that is best for you; your visa affects your legal and tax status.
- have all the documents you need and know how to fill them out (see below).
- understand what you can—and *cannot*—do when you get here.
- can get help if the rules or your situation changes.

Tax status

If you live or work here, you probably will pay U.S. taxes (see chapter on "Paying Your Taxes"). Unfortunately, U.S. tax rules are complicated—especially for foreign nationals. But you may be able to save time and money if you learn about U.S. tax rules *before* you leave. Ask an international tax professional:

- Will I pay U.S. taxes? Will I pay taxes to my own country, too?
- How much will I pay? When will I pay?
- What can I do to save money?
- What rules do I need to know before I leave?

Insurance

 Make sure you can get medical insurance *before* you come to the U.S. (see chapter on "Insurance"). In fact, many sponsors, schools, and employers will not let you come without insurance. If you are coming here to study or work, ask your school or company for help. If you are coming on your own, call a few companies that give insurance to internationals. Find out:

Often, the company, school, or organization that is sponsoring you can help. Many large organizations work with experts such as:

- immigration attorneys.
- tax professionals.
- insurance companies.
- international moving companies.

- how long you will wait. For example, with some companies, you wait six months or longer; you may need short-term insurance before your regular insurance begins.
- how long the insurance lasts. Be sure you can get insurance for the whole time you are here.
- how much the insurance costs. If your sponsor, school, or employer does not give you insurance, check with a few companies.

Cost of living

Make sure you can afford to live here. If you will be studying here, ask the school how much you will need in U.S. dollars for each month here. In fact, you will sign a paper showing you have enough (see chapter on "Colleges and Universities").

Banking information

To transfer money to the U.S., you will need to know your home bank's:

- routing number.
- address.
- account number (see chapter on "Money Matters").

Find out if your bank or a bank in your country has correspondent relationships with U.S. banks. When you are in the U.S., this relationship may help you get:

- a charge or credit card.
- emergency funds.
- a loan.

What to Bring

Money

- cash in U.S. dollars. Bring $150-$200 U.S. dollars for things you will need right away—for example, taxis, tips, and food. If you arrive on a weekend, you may want to bring $100 more; most banks are closed.
- traveler's checks. Issued in U.S. dollars, these can be used as cash; if they are lost or stolen, you may get new ones.

Charge or credit cards

Americans use credit and charge cards to buy everyday items such as food, clothing, movie and theater tickets (see chapter on "Credit Cards and Loans"). If you will be here for more than six months, you may save money if you use an American credit card—rather than one from your home country.

Your school, company, or organization may be able to get you a card right away. If not, get an American Express card in your home country. When you arrive in the U.S., you will be able to get a U.S. American Express card. After a few months, you will be able to get another credit card if you like.

Telephone calling card

You may need a calling card for international calls when you get to the U.S. Call a U.S. telephone service (see "Chapter Information" in the Appendix).

Documents

Entry papers.

- a passport for each family member 21 years or older. Check the expiration date on your passport(s); if it expires less than six months from the time you plan to enter the U.S., ask for an extension. Keep your passport valid at all times.
- a visa for each family member 21 years or older. One family member has the visa status of "principal employee" or "principal student." Other family members have "derivative status." The visa is stamped on the inside of your passport at the U.S. Consulate. The visa tells
  - the purpose of your visit.
  - the expiration date, or last date, you can enter the U.S.
  - how many times you can enter.

Financial information. You will need any documents that show your income and assets outside the U.S., including:

- a copy of your latest tax returns.

- the deed for any property you own in your home country.
- a letter from your bank giving your financial history. This may help you get a loan or a credit card—especially if your bank has a correspondent relationship with the U.S. bank.
- bank statements and records of any other assets.
- credit or loan documents.

Automobile information.

- international driver's license or the driver's license you are now using.
- "no-claim letter" (in English) from your car insurance company, showing that you are a safe driver. Sometimes, this letter reduces your car insurance payments in the U.S.
- car ownership records if you are bringing your car to the U.S., including your
  - bill of sale.
  - international registration marker.
  - car serial and motor numbers.

If you use the Internet, look up "Hello! America" (http://www.hellousa.com/world) for:

- books, information, and advice about U.S. cities and life.
- orientation services you can use before you leave and after you get here.
- choosing and applying to colleges.

Also, most large cities have a Chamber of Commerce on the World Wide Web; search under the name of the city. Many cities list entertainment news, travel information, and real estate agents on the Web.

– insurance policy records.

Medical records.

- immunizations.
- medicines you take.
- illnesses you have had.

Birth certificates. Bring originals (preferably translated into English and notarized).

Education records.

- transcripts.
- diplomas.
- test records (such as the TOEFL).

Job and professional records.

- reference letters (on company or university stationery).
- your résumé or curriculum vitae (CV).
- proof of your qualifications (see chapter on "Finding Work").

Legal papers.

 Have a certified translation of all legal papers.

- copies of will(s).
- proof of legal guardianship for any minor (child under the age of 18) who is accompanying you and is not your own child.

Copies of insurance policies.

Compare the cost of adding onto the health insurance you now have versus buying insurance in the U.S. (see "Insurance" above).

Inventory.

List all items packed, shipped, or stored.

Useful items

You may want:

- household medicine and antibiotics. In the U.S., you will need a prescription for many medicines (see chapter on "Medical Care"). Check with the U.S. Embassy or Consulate in your area about restrictions on bringing drugs to the U.S. (see chapter on "Your Legal Status").
- an extra pair of prescription eyeglasses.
- a thermometer for measuring degrees Celsius.
- extra photographs (headshots). The photos should be passport size. You need these for the many forms you will complete.
- extra luggage keys.

What to leave at home

Compare the cost of shipping or bringing an item versus buying it in the U.S. For example, compare:

- large items—such as furniture.
- everyday items—such as medicines, shoes, or clothing.

Clothing.

- heavy indoor clothing. Almost all homes and buildings have air conditioning and central heating, so indoor temperatures are about the same throughout the year.
- extra children's clothing. Children who move to the U.S. often want what American children wear; since clothing in the U.S. is often cheap, you may want to buy it here.

Electrical items. The electrical outlets and currents here are different from those in most countries. The U.S. electricity standard is 110-120 volt, 60 cycles AC. Before you come, be sure any appliances you bring will work here. Go to a store that knows about international equipment. Check your:

- appliances. Most large appliances will not work in the U.S.
- musical equipment, such as stereos.
- radios, TVs, and video and audio cassette players. American equipment uses the NTSC system to
  - get American radio stations or TV channels.
  - play American videos, audio cassettes, and CDs.

Most other countries use the PAL, SECAM, or MESELAM systems. If your equipment has only one system, you may need to convert it (see chapter on "News, Sports, & Entertainment").

Furniture. Furniture is usually cheaper in the U.S.—especially used furniture (see chapter on "Moving In"). You may want to:

- rent a furnished house or apartment.
- rent furniture.
- buy new furniture.

Cars. Any car brought into the U.S. must meet U.S. highway safety standards and have a working catalytic converter. You will also need specific automobile documents. You may save time and money if you buy or lease a car in the U.S. (see chapters on "Getting Around" and "Buying or Leasing a Car").

If you want to ship your car overseas, find out:

- the rules for your car. For example
  - you may not bring some cars in at all.
  - you may bring other cars in; but you will need to "fix it" so it meets U.S. standards.
- the fees for bringing the car into the country.
- the way to get new parts. You may not be able to get parts if
  - the type of car is not popular here.
  - the driver's seat is on the right side; U.S. drivers sit on the left.
- the type of gasoline it uses. Only cars that use unleaded gas can come in.

Bringing items into the U.S.

Ask the U.S. Consulate nearest you about bringing the items below.

Items from certain countries. You cannot import some items from Cambodia, Cuba, North Korea, or Vietnam.

Items needing a special permit.

- firearms and ammunition. Get a letter from your consulate before you bring in any weapon; the letter should state that this weapon is allowed.
- some drugs and medicines. Keep the medicine in the box or bottle from the drugstore. If possible, the box or bottle should have
  - the name of the medicine

- the name, address, and telephone number of your doctor.
- the name of the drugstore.
- plants and meat products, such as fruits, vegetables, seeds, and untanned animal furs or skins.

Gold coins, jewelry, and medals.
You can import only a certain amount of these items.

Pets.

- Have your pet examined by a veterinarian. U.S. Customs will not admit a pet that has any diseases it can transmit to humans. If you have a dog or cat, bring a health certificate from the veterinarian.
- Have dogs or cats three months or older vaccinated against rabies at least 30 days before coming to the U.S.
- Call your airlines; check the hours of operation at your port of arrival to be sure that an officer is available to inspect your pet when you arrive at U.S. Customs.
- Make plans for shipping your pet. Ask which kind of pet carrier you need.
- Label all pet carriers with
  - your name and address.
  - the name and address of anyone who will be picking up your pet.
  - a statement with the number of animals contained in each shipment.
- Check to be sure your hotel or housing allows pets.

International Movers

Moving companies

Talk to a few companies. Ask about:

- experience. Make sure the company has done many international moves from your home country to the U.S.
- reputation. Talk to at least three people who have used the company for U.S. moves. Make sure they were satisfied.
- insurance. Be sure the mover is bonded, or insured. Ask if the insurance covers all your belongings while they are on the ship.
- price. Get a written estimate (see below) from three or more companies. Find out what this price includes. For example, many larger companies help you
  - pack.
  - get the shipping documents ready.
  - arrange for Customs, or get permission to bring your items into the country.
  - unpack.
- special services. For example, the company may
  - help you get your appliances ready.
  - tell you about the taxes and rules for bringing in certain items (see below).
  - have booklets or videos about your new country.

Extra costs

Some costs that may not be in the estimate are:

- mattress bags and wardrobe boxes.
- extra pickups or deliveries.
- preparation of your electrical appliances.
- extra insurance for special items—such as antiques or jewelry.
- car shipment into the U.S. You may need to pay
  - taxes.
  - the cost of making your car meet government standards.
- fees and taxes for bringing some items into the U.S. For example you may need to pay for
  - antiques, or items over 100 years old; find out the rules and get a letter from an appraiser.
  - jewelry or furs. If you will wear these items yourself— rather than sell them—you may not need to pay.
- storage of your goods for awhile—either in your home country or the U.S.
- tips. If the service was satisfactory, you may tip each worker $5–$10 for each worker for a move that takes two days.

Your records

Write down:

- the transit time (how long it will take).
- the itemized cost estimate, or an "order for service." If possible,

get a "binding estimate" so the company cannot add extra costs.
- insurance. Be sure you know the amount of insurance in case of damage. You can also buy separate insurance from an insurance company.
- an inventory of each item to be moved; it should list each item separately and describe any damage or marks already on the items before the move begins.

 Be sure you know about any special procedures, restrictions, or taxes on taking possessions (such as a car) into your own country from the U.S.

If necessary, save receipts or proofs of purchase for items you bought here. These may include:

- cars.
- cameras.
- jewelry.

Words to Know

Antibiotic: a kind of medicine—for example, medicine for sore throats and other infections

Appliances: electrical items such as refrigerators, toasters, and irons

Assets: the property and money a person has

Bank statement: a paper that shows how much money you have in your bank account

Bill of sale: a paper that shows what you bought and how much you paid

Binding estimate: the amount the service costs. The company cannot charge you more than this amount.

Birth certificate: an official document that shows when and where a person was born

Bonded: insured in case a worker steals or breaks something

Car serial number: the identification number of a car—often on the dashboard or under the hood

Central heating: a heating system that heats the whole house—not just one room

Certified translation: translation with a legal stamp showing that it is accurate

Convert: change something (a video player or a machine). For example, you need to convert most foreign TVs so they will get American channels.

Correspondent (bank): having a special relationship with a bank from another country. For example, a bank in France may have a correspondent bank in the U.S.; if you are a customer of the French bank, you may be able to get faster and better service from the correspondent bank in the U.S.

Credit card: a plastic card used to buy things; you get the bill later

Curriculum vitae (CV): (see "Résumé")

Derivative status: the legal status for families of the principal student or employee

Drugstore: a pharmacy; a place where you can buy medicine

Expiration date: the date your visa ends

Extension: getting permission to stay longer

Firearms: guns and other weapons

Guardianship: having the legal responsibility to care for a child

Immunization: medicine or injection that keeps you from getting diseases

Inventory: a list of all items packed, shipped, or stored

Mattress bag: a plastic bag to cover a mattress

"No-claim letter": a letter from your car insurance company that shows you are a safe driver

Pet carrier: a strong box that holds pets while traveling

Principal employee: the employee who holds the visa for himself or herself and for the family

Principal student: the student who holds the visa for himself or herself and for the family

Qualification: the ability to do a job

Reference letter: a letter from your past employer that says you did a good job

Résumé: a CV; a document that describes your education, employment history, and qualifications

Routing number: a bank's identification number for international wire transfers; a bank's electronic address

Tax return: a document you send to the government each year. It shows how much money you made and the taxes you paid.

Transcript: a person's official school record that shows the classes taken and the grades received

Vaccinated: getting a shot or injection (see "Immunization" above)

Wardrobe box: a box movers use for clothes. The box lets you keep the clothes on hangers so they won't get wrinkled.

Will: an official document that shows who gets a person's money and property after he or she dies

__When You Arrive__

Sample VISA

Nº 000000

THE **UNITED STATES**
OF **AMERICA**
NONIMMIGRANT VISA
ISSUED AT

TUNIS

G - 4   19   FEB   1991
CLASSIFICATION   DATE ISSUED

VALID FOR   **MULTIPLE** ←——— Number of times you
                                       can leave and re-en-
APPLICATION FOR ENTRY   ter the country
UNTIL
18   FEB   1996 ↖

                              ←——— Expiration date:
BEARER(S)   check for accuracy
ISSUED TO

John P. Smithe

CONSULAR OFFICER   0000

__Dollars & Cents__

With $1.00 you can:
• buy one large chocolate chip cookie

With $5.00 you can:
• rent two videos for the night

With $10.00 you can:
• get a quick haircut

With $20.00 you can:
• buy a fancy T-shirt

With $50.00 you can:
• buy a pair of sneakers

With $100.00 you can:
• see a popular musical

A quarter = 25 cents (25¢)

**A penny =
1 cent (1¢)**

**A nickel =
5 cents (5¢)**

**A dime =
10 cents (10¢)**

_____Tipping_____

Occupation	Average Amount to Tip
Restaurants waiters/waitresses (except for employees at "fast-food" restaurants)	15% of food bill not including tax
Airports, Trains, or Bus terminals baggage handlers–porters who carry your luggage	$1.00–$2.00 per bag
Barber shops/Beauty salons hairdressers and barbers	15%
Taxis and Limos drivers	10%–15% of fare
Hotels room service (delivering food or laundry) porters door persons (who call a taxi for you)	50¢ – $1.00 $1.00 per bag 25¢-50¢

Do not tip:

- **officials** such as police officers or government employees.
- **service employees** such as bus drivers, theater ushers, museum guides, sales people, gas station attendants, elevator operators, receptionists.

Tips on Tipping

In general...

? *Are tipping customs the same all over the country?* No. Leave a larger tip (about 20%) in major cities such as New York and Los Angeles. You may leave about 15% in smaller cities or in the country—but not less than 15%.

? *Why should I tip?* Most waiters and other service people are paid less because they get tips. If you do not tip, you are cheating them out of money they earned.

? *Should I ever tip the employee of a store where I am shopping?* In general, no. For example, do not tip a salesperson—even if that person spent a lot of time helping you. Many salespeople get a commission—that is, a percentage of the price you pay.

Note: In some food stores, shoppers give 25¢–50¢ to a bagger who carries groceries to the car. Other grocery stores do not allow tips. Watch what other shoppers do.

? *What are the customs for tipping at holiday time?* (See chapter on "Making Friends").

Restaurants and Hotels

? *Should I tip the maitre d'?* Usually, no. Tip only if you receive extra attention—for example, if the maitre d' helped you get ready for a large party or special group.

? *Should I ever leave more than 15% of the bill?* Yes. The staff of a five-star hotel or restaurant usually expects about 20–25%. Also, large groups (six or more) usually leave 18–20%. Check to be sure the tip is not already on the bill.

? *May I leave a smaller tip if the service was not good?* Yes, but only if the service was unusually bad. Many Americans leave a little less than 15% and complain to the manager. If you leave a smaller tip, be sure that the problem was the fault of the service person—not the kitchen.

? *Should I ever leave no tip at all?* Do not leave a tip in cafeterias, or informal restaurants—such as McDonald's.

Taxi and Delivery Services

? *Should I tip the person who delivers pizza or other food to my home?* Yes, about 15%.

? *Should I tip the drivers for mail services, department stores, or flower shops?* No.

? *Should I tip the person who calls the cab for me?* Sometimes. Tip the hotel door person who catches a cab from the street. Usually, you need not tip the cab dispatcher at the airport or train station.

Quick Information

Arrival assistance

The Traveler's Aid Society (TAS) has a desk at most large airports. It is open 24 hours a day and helps with problems such as money and transportation.

Telephone

Read the chapter on "The Telephone" for more information about using the telephone.

Information service. You may get a telephone number by dialing Information from any phone; in most cities, you will pay a small fee for this service.

Dial "411" for local information.

Phone books. You may use:

- the White Pages for
  - the telephone numbers of homes and businesses.
  - entertainment information.
  - maps.
  - numbers for the local weather or the weather for any major U.S. city.
- the Yellow Pages for
  - the telephone number of a business.
  - advertisements of businesses.
- the government section for names and numbers of government offices.

Airport bookstore

All major airports have bookstores with books, magazines, and newspapers for the city. If you are staying for more than a few weeks, ask for a book that tells about *living* in the city (see chapter on "News, Sports, & Entertainment").

Tourist centers

Every major city has a tourist center. Often, someone can help you make reservations right at the center. Look in the Yellow Pages under "Tourist."

National Council for International Visitors (NCIV)

The NCIV may be able to:

- arrange tours.
- get a translator or interpreter.
- reserve a hotel.

Call the national number to find out if your city has a local organization that works with the NCIV (see chapter on "Making Friends" and "Chapter Information"—"Making Friends"—in the Appendix).

At the Airport

Entering the U.S.

Documents: When you enter the U.S., you will need to show the immigration officer your:

- visa, which is stamped inside your passport.
- I-94 card. The officer will attach this to your passport. Check to see how long you are permitted to stay in the U.S. If you need to stay longer, explain why you are coming to the U.S. and ask for an extension. Do not remove the card after you leave the airport.
- U.S. Customs declaration card.
- entry papers—such as the IAP-66 ("pink") form.

Transportation. Most large airports have transportation to the downtown area or the suburbs. You may take a:

- taxi. Tip the driver about 15% of the fare. In addition to the fare, the taxi may charge extra for
  - cach extra passenger.
  - luggage.
- shuttle service—either a van or a limousine. Shuttle services often cost less than taxis; but they may take longer, because they have other passengers to drop off.
- bus, subway, or train. Many airports—but not all—have public transportation into the city.
- rental car (see chapter on "Traveling In & Out of the U.S.").

Where to Stay

Hotels

Most hotels have:

- maid service.
- laundry service.
- room service.
- dining.

Some hotels offer:

- suites with small kitchens.
- free parking.
- bilingual staff members (see chapter on "Traveling In and Out of the U.S.").
- smoking and smoke-free rooms.

Motels

Motels are like hotels; but they are usually cheaper and have parking. Most motels are in the suburbs or by the road—rather than in the downtown area. Some motels have restaurants, small kitchens, washers and dryers, and pools.

Guest houses

You may rent a room at a guest house or Bed and Breakfast (B&B), for long- or short-term. Often, you share a bathroom with other guests. Some guest houses offer meals.

Temporary homes

You may rent a temporary home for one week, one month, or more. Most temporary homes come with everything you need—such as furniture, linens (sheets and towels), bedding, dishes, kitchen utensils, and appliances (see chapter on "Finding a New Home").

 In general, furnished apartments cost about 50% more than unfurnished apartments. You will pay a security deposit (about 1 month's rent) along with the first rent payment; you will get the money back when you leave. Find out which fees and services are included in the rent.

Services. Some short-term places offer special services that may be included in the rental price. For example, you may get:

- 24-hour front desk service.
- maid service.
- newspaper delivery.
- transportation to airports.

American Youth Hostels. Travelers of all ages stay here (see "Chapter Information"—"Traveling In & Out of the U.S."—in the Appendix). Usually, you share a bedroom and bathroom with other people. The cost is usually under $25 a night. You pay extra for sheets and blankets, towels, or meals. Members get discounts; the membership fee is about $25 a year.

Camping. The U.S. has many national and state parks where you can camp. Some camping grounds have cooking grills, toilets, and showers. Some campsites are free; others charge a fee—usually under $20 a night. You often need reservations.

Social Security

Employers, banks, and schools use the Social Security card for identification. If you cannot work, your Social Security card will say, "Not Valid for Employment." If you can work, your card will not have this message. Your employer should also check your other documents to be sure.

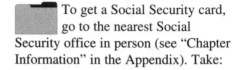 To get a Social Security card, go to the nearest Social Security office in person (see "Chapter Information" in the Appendix). Take:

- your passport with the I-94 card.
- immigration papers—such as the IAP-66 ("pink") form.
- completed SS-5 application form. You can get one at the Social Security office.

What to do first

1. **Find out what kind of help you can get from your employer or sponsor.**

2. **Have all official documents translated into English.**

All translations should be notarized by a notary public or authenticated by your country's embassy. You will pay a small fee. You must show some form of identification—such as a driver's license or a passport. You can find a notary public at:

- banks and law offices.
- most real estate offices.
- some translation companies.

3. **Apply for a Social Security card.**

4. **Open a bank account (see chapter on "Money Matters").**

You probably will need a checking account to rent a home. You may rent a safe-deposit box for all valuables.

5. **Find out about schools if you have children.**

The public school your child goes to depends on the area where you live (see chapter on "Your Older Child").

6. **Find a place to live.**

Pay the deposit with a check.

Getting Settled

Once you have taken care of your immediate needs:

- register your child(ren) at a school.
- get a driver's license (see chapter on "Getting Around").
- get insurance for
  - health care.
  - personal property.
  - your car.
- make a list of emergency telephone numbers—for example, fire, police, and hospitals (see "Help!"—"In an Emergency"—in the Appendix).

- find a family doctor.
- arrange for visa extensions or work permission for dependents.

Translation Services

Examples of official documents you may need translated are:

- school records.
- medical records.
- birth certificates.
- a license to practice a certain profession.

The translation may take from one day to several weeks depending on the language and the number of words. Most agencies will offer a "rush" service if you need it quickly; but prices are higher.

Most translation companies estimate the cost of translating a document per every thousand words, but some companies may charge by the word or page. The price of the whole document also depends on the:

- languages used. The more common languages usually cost less.
- type of document. For example, a document with a lot of technical language dealing with specific subject matter (such as medical or legal terms) will be more expensive.
- number of words. Usually, there is a minimum cost for any document, regardless of its length. You may be able to get a cheaper rate for longer documents.

What to look for

A general cost estimate. Remember that most companies do not give estimates before they see the document.

Notarized documents. Some companies can notarize documents, or put on a legal stamp, if necessary.

Extra help in case the translation or the service is not satisfactory.

Client references or sample translations.

Other services

Translation companies may sometimes also offer other language services, such as:

- interpretation services for help with speaking or listening at conferences, meetings, and seminars. You may also hire an interpreter to guide you around the area.
- audio tape transcriptions for transcribing (writing) a recorded tape in a foreign language or from one language to another.
- videotape dubbing for recording voices in any language over a film.
- language instruction.

Telephone translation services

All the major long-distance phone companies offer translation services. For example, AT&T can translate from Japanese to English, Spanish to Ko-

rean, or from Chinese Mandarin to Hebrew. To find out about this service, call AT&T, MCI, or Sprint (see "Chapter Information"—"Telephone Services and Equipment"—in the Appendix). To use this service you must be able to say in English:

- your name.
- the language you speak.
- the number you want to call.
- your card number and expiration date if you will be billed through your credit card.
- your home telephone number if you are living in the U.S.

Ask about the different plans. For example, if you have a credit card from a major bank, you may pay for each call with your card. With another plan, you pay the telephone company each month for a certain number of calls; you do not need a credit card.

You may need to pay a "subscription fee" of $200 or more to sign up for the service. The cost of each phone call depends on:

- the language you speak.
- the amount of time you are on the phone.
- the time of day you call.

If you talk for four minutes, the phone call may be about $30 or less. If you talk for 30 minutes, the cost may be almost $200.

You need to speak English well to start this service. Someone who speaks English must call ahead of time to start the service.

Words to Know

Authenticate: to stamp a document. The stamp shows the document is true.

Bilingual: speaking two languages

Concierge: a person who works at the front desk of a hotel or apartment building

Customs inspection station: the place at the airport where officers see what is in your baggage

Customs declaration card: a card you get on the airplane. You write what you are bringing into the U.S.

Dependent: a person who gets a visa as a family member (such as a husband, wife, or child) or a certain type of employee (such as the driver of a diplomat)

Dubbing: recording voices in any language over a film or videotape

Extension: a written agreement from the Immigration and Naturalization Service (INS) that lets you stay in the country longer

Guest house: a house where you can rent a room for a short or long time

I-94 card: a card that an immigration officer attaches to your passport

Interpreter: a person who repeats someone else's words in another language

Limousine: a large car, also called a "limo"

Motel: a kind of hotel. Each room has a door to the outside and comes with a parking space.

Notarize: to make a document legal; to put an official stamp on a document

Notary public: a person who helps to make a document legal. A notary public signs that a signature is true.

Security deposit: the money you pay the owner of the house or apartment before you rent it

Social Security card: a U.S. government card with an identification number—needed to work legally in the U.S.

Suite: a group of rooms in a hotel

Temporary home: a house you can rent for a short or long time

Traveler's Aid Society (TAS): a place at the airport that helps travelers

White Pages: the telephone book that lists people's names, addresses, and home numbers

Yellow Pages: the telephone book that has advertisements for products and services and business phone numbers. You look up the name of a product or service to find out where to buy it.

Youth hostel: a place to stay while you are on a trip. Usually, you share a bedroom and bathroom with other people.

___The Telephone___

Local Calls

Dial:
- the 7-digit number.

Do not dial the area code if you are calling the same area code and the number is in your local calling area.

example:
461-4980

Long-Distance Calls

Dial:
- "1".
- the area code.
- the 7-digit number.

example:
1-912/344-0199

International Calls

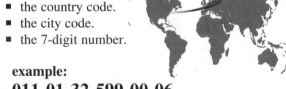

Dial:
- "011".
- the country code.
- the city code.
- the 7-digit number.

example:
011-01-32-599-00-06

Operator-Assisted Calls

Dial:
- "0" for operator assistance in the U.S.
- "01" for international assistance in areas with direct dialing.
- "00" for international assistance in areas without direct dialing.

Dial "0"

An operator can help with collect calls, person-to-person calls, calling card calls, emergency calls, and general problems.

Information Calls

Dial:
- "411" for local information.
- "1" + the area code + "555-1212" for long-distance information.

example:1-215/555-1212

Making Phone Calls

Calling the number

Every U.S. number has a 3-digit area code and a 7-digit number.

For example, in the number 212/223-9000:

- "212" is the area code.
- "223-9000" is the number.

Local numbers. For most local calls, dial only the 7-digit number. You may need to dial the 3-digit area code for some local calls in large metropolitan areas—such as San Francisco and Washington DC. The White Pages has a list of the local exchanges.

Most local calls have no extra charges, unless you call from a pay phone (see "Pay Phones" below and "Ordering Phone Service" in chapter on "Telephone Services and Equipment").

Note: You may need to dial: "9" or "8" to get an "outside line" if you are calling from a campus or office building.

Long-distance calls. Dial "1" + the area code and the number.

Phone numbers with letters. Some business numbers have letters instead of numbers. Press the letters on the phone buttons; for example, the number 212/PHONE-US is the same as 212/746-6387.

"800" and "888" numbers. Many business numbers start with "800" or "888." These are toll-free; that is, your call to them is free—even if the office is not in the local area. Dial "1" + "800" or "888" and the number.

"900" numbers. If you call a number with "900," "915," or "976," you pay extra for the call. Sometimes these numbers cost $7 a minute or more. Dial "1" + "900" and the number.

What if I have an emergency and the number I call is busy? Dial or press "0." Ask the operator to interrupt the call for you.

What if a recorded voice answers and tells me something I don't understand? Recorded messages are more and more common in the U.S. The voice tells you which number to press; for example, if you call a theater, the message might say to "press '1' for more information on showtimes" or "'2' to order tickets." If you do not understand the recording, try one of the following to talk to someone:

- Wait; do not press any buttons. Usually, someone will answer the call.
- Dial or press "0." Sometimes, you will get an operator.

For an emergency, dial "911."

- Dial "1" or any other number you hear; after you have pressed a few times, someone may answer; explain what you need and the person will connect you to the right line.

Finding a number

Local. You may:

- call "411." You may be charged about 12¢–36¢ each time you call from a phone at your home or office. You may need 25¢ if you call "411" from a pay phone; in some areas, you will get the money back.
- use the telephone book (see "Telephone Books" below).

Long distance. To get the area code:

- find the U.S. map in the front pages of the White or Yellow Pages (see chapter on "Telephone Service and Equipment"). Look up the area code on the map.
- dial "0" for operator. Give the name of the city or town and the state you want.

To get the rest of the number dial long-distance information—that is, "1 + the area code + 555-1212" (see first page of this chapter).

In most cities, you can make about 10–15 "411" calls and 3 long-distance information calls in one month. Then you will pay for all long-distance information calls—local, long-distance within the U.S., and international.

Long-distance Calls

Services. If you just moved into a new home, get a long-distance service right away (see "Ordering Phone Service" in chapter on "Telephone Services & Equipment"). If you have just come to the U.S. and do not have a private phone to use, find a:

- pay phone. You may need a credit or calling card; pay phones do not take dollar bills.
- telephone center where you can make international calls; you may pay with cash.

The cost for a long-distance call is different for each long-distance service. It may also depend on the time when you call—for example:

- 8 am–4:59 pm, Monday-Friday ("daytime"): most expensive.
- 5 pm–10:59 pm, Sunday-Friday ("evening"): less expensive.
- 11 pm–7:59 am, Monday-Friday, all day Saturday, and Sunday until 4:59 pm ("night/weekend"): least expensive.

How can I tell if a number is long-distance? Most numbers are local if they are in the same city or town. To find out if a number is long-distance, you may:

- dial "0" and ask the operator.
- dial the number. If you make the connection without dialing "1" the number is local; if it is long-distance, you will get a message.

- look up the first 3 digits in the front part of the phone book. The White Pages or Yellow Pages has a list of the three digits at the beginning of all local numbers.

? ***What if I dial the wrong number on a long-distance call?*** Dial "0" and tell the operator you got the wrong number. In most places, you will get your money back.

? ***What if the phone connection is not good?*** Dial "0" and tell the operator you got a "bad connection." The operator will dial the number for you.

Calling cards. All the major long-distance services can give you a calling card. With calling cards:

- you may call from any phone. For example, you can call from a pay phone or from a friend's phone; the bill will go to your home.
- you do not need money; the company will send a bill to your home.
- you may save money from a hotel. Most hotels charge extra for long-distance calls. With a calling card, you may save that extra cost.

Time zones. Be aware of the differences in time when you are calling another part of the U.S. (see first page of chapter on "Traveling In & Out of the U.S.").

International Calls

For instructions, see first page of this chapter.

 To save money:

- dial direct; that is, do not use the operator. Dial "011" + the country code + the city code + the number. Calls made without an operator are called station-to-station calls.
- ask each long-distance company about its discounts.
- ask your long-distance company what time of day is best.

Operator-assisted Calls

An operator can help you make a local or long-distance call. Dial:

- "0" for calls in the U.S., then the number. The operator will answer after you have dialed.
- "01" for international calls in areas with direct international dialing, then the number. The operator will answer after you have dialed.
- "00" for international calls to areas without direct international dialing. Wait for the operator to answer.
- Operator-assisted calls are $2–$7 more than station-to-station calls.

Collect calls. The person you are calling pays for the call. To make a collect call, dial "0" + area code + number. An operator will make the connection for you. The operator will ask if the person you are calling will accept the charges, or cost, for the call.

Person-to-person calls. Dial "0" + area code + number. Tell the operator the name of the person you want to talk to. If the person is not there, the operator does not connect you and does not charge for the call.

Third-number billing. To charge your long-distance call to another number, dial "0" + the area code + the number. Tell the operator you want to "charge the call to another number." Then give your home number.

"Translation" calls. You may have someone translate any phone call for you (see chapter on "When You Arrive").

Pay Phones

You can find pay phones:

- on most main streets—especially near gas stations.
- in most malls and restaurants—especially near the rest rooms.

You may call any U.S. or international number from a pay phone. Use coins (nickels, dimes or quarters) for local calls. You need a calling card for most long-distance calls (see "Long-distance Calls" above).

Local calls. Local calls in most cities cost 25¢ for three minutes. Use exact change; extra money is not returned.

What if I lose money in a pay phone? Dial "0" for operator. For example, say, "I put two quarters in the machine. I dialed the number, but the line was busy. When I hung up, I didn't get my money back." The operator may dial the number again for you.

Telephone Books

You can find telephone books in most hotel rooms and near many pay phones. Use:

- the Yellow Pages for the numbers of stores and services. This book has
  - an alphabetical list of different kinds of services—such as "Airlines," "Computers," and "Schools."
  - a sublist under many services—such as "Schools— Elementary and Secondary" or "Schools—Pre-School and Kindergarten."
  - the names of each service listed alphabetically.
  - advertisements that different services have paid for.
- the White Pages for the numbers of homes, businesses, and government offices.

Other phone book information. The front of the telephone book has information such as:

- telephone rates and kinds of services.
- information on using the telephone.
- emergency numbers.

- U.S. maps with area codes.
- local maps of the subway and city streets.
- numbers you can call to get the time and weather; you can get the weather for any major U.S. city.
- information on sports and cultural events (see chapter on "News, Sports, and Entertainment").

The White Pages or Yellow Pages gives the telephone numbers of government offices; often these pages are a different color. To find a government office, find the government level (city, county, state, and U.S. or federal). Then find the department. For example, for the number of your local post office, look up "U.S. Government." Then find "Postal Service" for a list of all the local post offices.

Words to Know

"800" and "888" numbers: free calls. You may call any "800" or "888" number for free (see "Toll-free numbers" below).

"900" number: a kind of telephone number. You pay for each minute of the call.

Answering machine: a machine that takes phone messages

Area code: the 3-digit code for the region where you live—for example, "212" for New York City.

Collect: a long-distance call that "reverses the charges." The person you are calling pays for the call.

Country code: a number you dial to call a country. Each country has its own code.

Dial tone: the humming sound you hear when you pick up the receiver

Exchange: the first three digits in a telephone number—after the area code. For example, in the number "913/944-0199," the digits "944" are the exchange.

Information: the number you dial to get someone's telephone number—dial "411"

Local: in the area where you do not pay extra for a call

Long-distance: not in the "free" area for your phone service

Outside line: line you use to reach a number outside a campus, office building, or hotel

Person-to-person: a kind of long-distance call. You tell the operator the name of the person you want to talk to. If the person is not there, the operator does not put the call through.

Receiver: a part of the phone. You hold the receiver in your hand.

Station-to-station: a kind of long-distance call. You speak to anyone who answers.

Toll-free ("800" and "888") numbers: free calls. You can call any "800" or "888" number for free.

White Pages: the telephone book that lists people's names and home numbers

Yellow Pages: the telephone book that has advertisements for products and services

Your Legal Status

Social Security Card

Overview

You need a visa to come to the U.S. to visit or live. You can get a(n):

- immigrant visa to live and work in the U.S. permanently.
- non-immigrant visa to live in the U.S. for awhile and then go back to your home country.

What is a "green card" or a "pink card"? A "green card" shows that you have immigrant status; that is, you can live and work here as long as you want (see "Immigrant Visas" below); after you have been here for five years, you may apply to become a citizen. The new cards from the INS are pink.

What is a "white card"? A "white card" shows that you have refugee status; that is, you left your country to escape persecution. You can live and work here as long as you want. You may also get immigrant status and apply to become a citizen.

The Federal Information Center has books and pamphlets on applying for jobs in the federal government, federal income taxes, immigration services, Social Security benefits, and other federal agencies, programs, and services. (see "Chapter Information" in the Appendix).

Immigrant Visas

Who can come

Family members. Most likely, you will be able to get a visa easily if a U.S. citizen is in your "immediate family"—that is, if you are the:

- husband or wife of a U.S. citizen.
- unmarried son or daughter of a U.S. citizen. You must be 21 years or younger.
- parent of a U.S. citizen. Your son or daughter must be over 21 years old.

You may also apply if the U.S. citizen is not in your "immediate family"— that is, if you are the:

- married son or daughter of a U.S. citizen.
- brother or sister of a U.S. citizen.

Many times, members who are not in the "immediate family" of a U.S. citizen wait years to get a visa.

Others. You may also apply if you:

- have a permanent job waiting for you; most often, you must be an expert in the arts or sciences—for example, a well-known musician, writer, artist, or engineer; some professionals need a license.
- are a refugee; that is, you left your country to escape persecution.

What your visa means

With an immigrant visa you may:

- travel anywhere in the U.S.
- leave the U.S. and return again as many times as you want.
- live here as long as you want.
- get a job here.
- apply to bring a member of your "immediate family" into the country.
- apply to be a citizen after you have lived here for five years (three years if you came here as

the husband or wife of a U.S. citizen).

Non-immigrant Visas

Who can come

If you have a visa to live and work here, you probably can get a visa for others in your family—that is, for:

- a husband or wife.
- an unmarried son or daughter, 21 years or younger.

What your visa means

Your visa lets you:

- come into the U.S.
- travel anywhere in the U.S.

Your visa shows:

- if you can work (see chapter on "Finding Work"); often, the principal can work but the family member cannot. For example, a person with an L1 visa can work; but the husband or wife with an L2 visa cannot.
- how long you can stay—most often, six months to seven years. Often, you apply for an extension from the Immigration and Naturalization Service (INS) in order to stay longer.
- how many times you can leave the U.S. and come back again. If you have questions about traveling outside the U.S., call the U.S. Embassy or Consulate in your home city.

Getting a Visa

Often, the company, school, or organization sponsoring you may be able to help.

U.S. Embassy or Consulate. Call the U.S. Embassy or Consulate in your home country.

The Immigration and Naturalization Service (INS). If you are in the U.S., you probably will send the first forms to an INS office in this country. Call the nearest INS number; you may get the number from the telephone book (see chapter on "When You Arrive"). Find the number in the U.S. Government section under:

- Justice (Department of).
- Immigration and Naturalization Service.

Professional help. If you have many questions about what to do and what forms you need, the INS office or the U.S. Embassy may not be able to help. You may get help from:

- attorneys. Find someone who has experience and training in immigration law (see "Choosing an Attorney" below).
- the organization bringing you here. If you are getting a non-immigrant visa, ask your sponsor, school, or employer.

To find out about other forms you need, see chapters on "Before You Come" and "When You Arrive."

Types of Visas

A visa: foreign government officials and employees such as ambassadors, public ministers, or career diplomatic or consular officers

B visa: people coming for a short while—usually less than one year

> B-1: people coming here to do business. Find out from an attorney or from the U.S. Embassy or Consulate what kinds of business you can and cannot do.
> B-2: tourists

E visa: treaty-traders and treaty-investors who want to trade with the U.S.

F visa: students in U.S. colleges, universities, seminaries (religious schools), language programs

G visa: representatives of international governmental organizations—such as the World Bank or the United Nations

H visa: people who will be here a certain amount of time—usually from 3–6 years. Most have a bachelors degree from a university.

- H-1: experts in business, science, or the arts—such as engineers, architects, teachers, or lawyers
- H-2: people who have temporary jobs in specific fields
- H-3: people in training programs

J visa: students, researchers, professors, and teachers—such as scientists for the National Institutes of Health. Usually, they are part of a U.S. government exchange program. After you finish the program, you may need to return to your home country for two years before you can come back.

K visa: men or women engaged to marry U.S. citizens (and their children)

L visa: employees who are transferred to the U.S. Usually, they:

- are professionals such as executives, managers, or technical specialists.
- are employees of large companies with offices in other countries.
- have worked for the company at least one year.

M visa: students at a vocational school to prepare for a job. The school cannot be a language school, a college, or a university.

Avoiding Common Problems

How to plan ahead

1. Check your papers.

Be sure the officials have filled out your papers correctly (see chapter on "Before You Come"). If you find an error—for example, an incorrect date—you may want to see an attorney right away.

2. Keep a calendar of the important dates right after you arrive.

For example, write the dates when you:

- are leaving the country.
- need an extension.
- are changing your status.

Also write the dates when you should see an attorney or contact the INS. This will save you a lot of time.

3. See an attorney, your school advisor, or your company contact about three months after you arrive—even if you think you have no problems.

For example, an attorney will talk about your future plans and look over your visa (see "Choosing an Attorney" below). Many attorneys will give you a free first visit.

Common problems

 Changing your visa may take two months or a year; every case is different. To be safe, begin as soon as you know about a problem or a possible change.

Errors on visa/papers (see "How to plan ahead" above).

Changes in status. Find out what to do if:

- you are changing jobs. Check with an attorney or other professional—even if you will be working for the same employer. For example, exchange visitors may have to fill out some forms to change from research to clinical work.
- you are changing schools. Go to the school's international office or the person in charge of the I-20 process at your new school.
- you are finishing your studies and going to work. Check with your employer's attorney to make sure you are authorized to work before you begin.
- you are getting married or divorced.

Extensions. To get an extension, you will need:

- an application to "Extend Time of Temporary Stay"; you may need either the I-129 or the I-539 (or both forms).
- I-94 forms for you, your spouse, and your children.

- other documents. The documents you need depend on the reason you want to stay longer; for example, you may need a letter from your employer if you are staying for work.
- the application fee.

You may call the INS (see "Getting a Visa" above) or an attorney. Getting an extension often takes about 30-45 days. Often the grace period is about 240 days as soon as you file; that is, you have 240 days after you file to get your extension approved. But special problems can cause the process to take longer or the grace period to be delayed. Start *at least* three months ahead of time.

? *Should I carry my passport around?* No. Take it only when you need identification papers; for example, you probably will need your passport to get a local driver's license.

? *Should I get a Social Security card?* Some newcomers—such as diplomats—do not need a social security card; but some lawyers say that everyone should have one for different forms and applications. For example, you need your Social Security number to apply to school, get a loan, or get a job.

Choosing an Attorney

Attorneys. To find an attorney:

- ask your embassy for recommendations.

- call the American Immigration Lawyers Association (see "Chapter Information" in the Appendix).
- talk to an attorney before you hire him or her. Again, many attorneys will not charge you for your first visit.

Visa services. Before you choose a visa service, ask:

- how much the service charges.
- what the service will do.
- how long the service has been in business.

Also ask for the names of references you can call.

 Some visa services charge a lot of money for doing some things you can do on your own. Others have been charged with fraud or illegal practices. Be careful when choosing a service!

Words to Know

American Immigration Lawyers Association: a group that represents lawyers who practice immigration law

Attorney: a person who represents you in business and law

Exchange visitor program: a program in which two people from different countries trade jobs

Extension: a written agreement that allows you more time to be in the country after a visa runs out

Fraud: a dishonest act, usually in business or law

"Green card" or "pink card": a paper, or document, that shows that you have an immigrant status; that is, you can live and work here as long as you want

"Immediate family": a father or mother, unmarried son or daughter under the age of 21, or husband or wife. Members of a U.S. citizen's immediate family are the most likely to get immigrant visas.

Immigrant visa: a visa that lets you live and work here as long as you want. You get an immigrant visa if you do not plan to live in your home country again.

Immigration and Naturalization Service (INS): the U.S. Government agency responsible for monitoring who comes into the country and how long they can stay

Non-immigrant visa: a visa that lets you live here for awhile—usually six months to five years. Non-immigrant visas are for people who will live in their home country again.

Persecution: actions against you because of your race, political ideas, religion, or nationality. Refugees come to the U.S. because their governments have persecuted them.

Principal: the student or employee who gets the visa; family members are dependents.

Refugee: a person who has come to the U.S. to escape persecution

"White card": a paper, or document, that shows that you have refugee status; that is, you left your country to escape persecution. You have the same rights as immigrants with a "green card" or "pink card."

Traveling In & Out of the U.S.

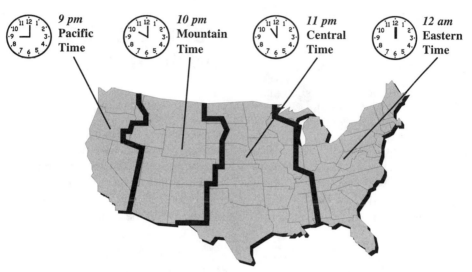

9 pm Pacific Time

10 pm Mountain Time

11 pm Central Time

12 am Eastern Time

Midnight —————————————— **Washington DC**

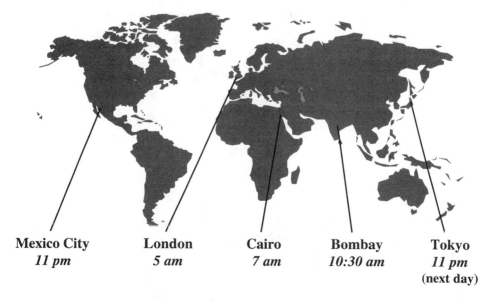

Mexico City
11 pm

London
5 am

Cairo
7 am

Bombay
10:30 am

Tokyo
11 pm
(next day)

Renting a Car

American highways are usually well-kept. When you plan your trip, try to stay away from big cities during the rush hours. If traffic is light, you can get from:

- New York City to Washington DC—4½–5 hours.
- Atlanta to Miami—12 hours.
- Dallas to Houston—9 hours.

 You pay less if you pump the gas yourself (see chapter on "Getting Around").

On some major highways, you will pay tolls; most are under $2 each. For example, in 1996, you would have paid about $10–$12 in tolls to drive from Washington DC to New York City.

 You must be at least 25 years old to rent a car.

You will need an international driver's license and a license from your home country.

 Prices vary according to the type of car, the company, and the city. Ask at the desk about discounts. The price per day will be less if you rent a car:

- for the whole week.
- on the weekend.

Gasoline. The car you get will have a full tank of gas. If you do not return it with a full tank, you pay for the gas you used. The price per gallon is often higher than the price at a gas station.

Insurance. You may already have insurance with your auto policy. You may get more insurance coverage from the auto-rental company; but be sure you need any insurance you pay for.

Note: You can buy a CD-ROM that maps out the best routes between all major cities. Look in computer and travel book stores.

Riding Buses and Trains

Buses

Taking a bus is usually less expensive than other ways you can travel; but buses often take longer because they stop in many places. Call and ask about express service. (see "Chapter Information" in the Appendix).

 The 1996 cost of some one-way trips are:

- $99 from Chicago to Houston—24 hours.
- $69 from Miami to Atlanta. 15½ hours.
- $35 from Los Angeles to San Francisco—10 hours.

 To get the lowest fares for trips over 800 miles, reserve tickets as soon as you can. Some bus companies have special discount programs.

Trains

Amtrak is the only train that goes to all parts of the U.S. All AMTRAK trains have a café or dining car; some have sleeping cars. (see "Chapter Information" in the Appendix).

You can buy tickets at the station or by phone with a credit card. The times for some 1996 one-way trips are:

- Chicago to Houston—27½ hours.
- Miami to Atlanta—23 hours (not a direct trip).
- Los Angeles to San Francisco—7 hours.

 To buy tickets in advance, call any Amtrak station or 1-800/ USA-RAIL (1-800/872-7245). If you want to tour the country by train, find out about Amtrak's discount passes such as:

- All Aboard America.
- the International USA Railpass for international visitors and residents.

Flying

Buying the tickets

You may buy tickets through a travel agent or directly from an airline. Get the tickets as soon as you can; you may get a discount for an advance purchase. Before you buy the tickets, find out if they are refundable, or if you can cancel the flight and get your money back.

Some cities have shuttles over popular, short routes. For example, you may take a shuttle from Washington DC to New York City or New York City to Boston. The shuttle flies every hour; you do not have to reserve your flight in advance.

The airport

Allow extra time to get to the airport if you are traveling around the time of a major holiday. Check with the airline to see when you should arrive.

Baggage. If you have a lot of luggage, call the airline ahead of time and ask:

- how many bags you can take; most airlines allow 2–3 bags per person.
- how many bags can be "carry-on."
- how much the bags can weigh.
- how big the bags can be.

Parking. Most airports have parking in:

- short-term lots. These may cost $5 an hour or more.
- long-term lots. These may be far away from the terminal; a shuttle bus will take you from the parking lot to the terminal for free.

Getting Ready

Money

Traveler's checks. Get them from your bank, an American Express office, or a foreign exchange office.

A major credit card. Write down the number of your credit card in case it is lost or stolen. Carry it separately from your credit cards.

Automatic teller machine bank card (ATM). You may use an ATM in most areas of the U.S.

Travel insurance

You may buy travel insurance from:

- travel agents.
- health insurance companies.
- travel insurance companies.

Trip cancellation or interruption insurance. You may have to cancel your trip because of an emergency—such as the illness or death of a family member. Cancellation/interruption insurance will give you back any fees you have already paid for the trip.

Medical assistance insurance is for accidents or illnesses that happen on the trip. Check with your insurance company to see if you are already insured while traveling; ask what you should do if you need to see a doctor in another area of the U.S. or in another country.

 When you arrive, put any valuables—such as jewelry, camera equipment, airplane tickets, and extra money—in a hotel safe-deposit box. Never leave your camera or any other costly item in the room; always carry it with you. Be especially careful in large cities and on beaches. Do not let go of the valuables you carry—even for a minute.

Leaving the country

Your passport. Make a photocopy of your passport. Carry it separately in case the passport is lost or stolen.

Before you leave:

- Check your visa status. Your visa shows if you can get into the U.S. again.

- Find out if you need new entry papers. For example, anyone with a J-1 visa may need another IAP-66 ("pink") form to re-enter the country.
- Inform the school's international students' office if you are a student.

How to leave your home

1. **Arrange for someone to take care of your home.**

Have a friend or neighbor watch your house or apartment while you are away. It is not impolite to ask someone who lives close to you—even if you do not know that person very well.

Keep lights on at all times or use a timer that turns the lights on or off; you can get a timer at a hardware store. Close all curtains and blinds.

2. **Ask your newspaper carriers and post office to hold deliveries while you are away.**

For short trips, ask a neighbor to pick up your newspaper and mail every day.

3. **Get a pet-sitter or take your pets to a kennel.**

A petsitter is a person who comes to your home and takes care of your pets while you are away.

4. Get your home ready.

Unplug all heating appliances and electronic equipment if you will be away for a long time; this will protect them from fire. Do not unplug your refrigerator or freezer.

If the temperature may go below freezing while you are gone, "winterize" your home. For example, you may need to protect the pipes from freezing. Ask your neighbors or the owner of the home what to do.

5. Tell the neighbors you will be away.

Ask them to call the police or fire department in case of emergency or if they see a stranger near your house. Leave a phone number where they can reach you.

Words to Know

Advance purchase: buying tickets in advance, or ahead of time

Airline: a company that owns and flies airplanes—such as TWA, Delta Air Lines, or British Airways

Automatic teller machine (ATM): a machine for transactions such as depositing and withdrawing money

"Carry-on": bags you can take with you on the plane

Compact car: the smallest sized car—usually for 3–4 people

Long-term parking lot: a place near the airport where you can park your car for more than one day

Luxury car: the largest sized car

Medical assistance insurance: insurance that pays for your medical care during a trip

Rush hour: the time of day when most people are driving to or coming home from work

Safe-deposit box: a safe for keeping valuables and important papers

Sedan: a mid-sized car—usually for 4–5 people

Short-term parking lot: an airport lot. Short-term parking is more expensive than long-term.

Shuttle: a flight that goes every hour. You do not have to reserve a seat. You may pay on the plane.

Shuttle bus: a bus that goes back and forth from the parking lot to the main part of the airport

Toll: money paid for using some roads and bridges

Trip cancellation insurance: insurance that pays for your trip if you cannot go or have to come home early

"Winterize": get the house ready for winter

__Getting Around__

Rules of the Road

 Drive on the right. Pass on the left.

 Stop for a red light. In some cities, you may take a right turn at a red light if no one is coming; but first look for the "No Turn on Red" sign.

Stop for a flashing red light; look around and then go ahead slowly.

Go slowly for a yellow light.

 Stop for a stopped school bus with flashing lights. You must stop if you are:

- in back of the bus.
- facing the bus in the opposite lane.

Wait for the bus to turn off the flashing lights and start again. Then you may go.

 In some states, the driver and any other person in the front seat must wear a seat belt—by law. Children under five years of age must sit in a child safety seat or wear a seat belt.

SEAT BELT

 The police have the right to stop your car and test your breath for alcohol. If you have been drinking, you may;

- lose your license.
- pay a fine.
- go to jail.

 Carry your driver's license and car registration card whenever you are driving. Keep the car registration in your wallet—not in the car—in case your car is stolen.

Driver's License

Public Transportation

Railway systems

Subways. Many metropolitan areas have a rail system that runs through the city and suburbs—for example:

- the "T" in Boston, MA.
- the BART in San Francisco, CA.
- the Metrorail in Miami, FL.

In most cities, you will not wait more than 15 minutes for a train.

Rail. You may also find commuter trains that go far out into the suburbs and to smaller cities—for example, in the Miami-Dade County and the San Francisco-Peninsula areas.

Buses

Some cities and suburbs have buses that go through the city or connect with the rail system.

 If you do not drive, find a place to live that is near a subway or bus. Make sure the train, subway, or bus runs:

- on the weekends.
- at times that are good for you.

Transfers

In most cities, you may get a transfer to go from a railway to a bus or from a bus to a bus. Transfers may be free or they may cost a small fee.

Discounts

Some people get discounts—for example:

- senior citizens (people over 65 years old).
- people who ride the subway or bus every day or who buy tickets for many trips at one time.

Taxis

Taxi drivers should have a license with a photo identification (ID) in a place where you can see it. You may get a cab:

- on the streets of many large cities. Look for a taxi with the roof light on and wave your hand.
- at hotels, airports, and rail stations.
- at your home. All cities have cabs that will pick you up at your door—even if you are in the suburbs. Most often, you will not pay extra. Usually, the taxi will come in about 15–20 minutes, but you cannot be sure; in bad weather or on Fridays, you may wait longer. If you know you will need a cab, call 1–2 days before you go.

 The cost depends on:

- the city. The taxis in each city charge different prices.
- the distance you go.
- the number of people in the taxi.
- the time of day; rush hour is most expensive.

In most cities, every taxi has a meter. Ask about the cost of the ride before you get in. Other cities have taxi zones; the cost of the trip changes as you go through each zone. Ask to see a map with the zones on it.

Parking

 Look for "No Parking" signs when you park on the street. Check the number of hours you can park. Be careful—especially in the city. If you get a ticket, you may pay a fine—sometimes over $100—or your car may be towed away.

Places to park

Garages. Garage parking in the city costs about $3–$5 an hour, or $15–$20 a day. Parking may be cheaper on Saturday and Sunday or at night.

Visitors' lots. If you are parking near a university or large office building, look for the signs that say "Visitors" or "Guest Parking." These parking lots are free.

Meters. Usually, you can put quarters in a parking meter; some meters also take dimes and nickels. Usually, you cannot park at meters during rush or peak hours (Monday–Friday, 7–9:30 am and 4–6:30 pm). In most places, you may park for free:

- after 6:30 pm.
- on Sundays.
- on holidays.

Parking validation. At some restaurants, stores, or movie theaters, you can park for free when you shop or

buy something. Ask someone in the shop to validate, or "stamp," your parking ticket. Give the ticket to the parking attendant when you leave.

Service Stations

 The price of gas depends on the time of year, the kind of gas, and the place you buy it. If you are using self-service, you may have to pay for the gas before you pump it.

Some stations will give you a discount for paying with:

- cash.
- the station's credit card.

Full service. The attendant will pump the gas, wipe the windshield, and check the oil, if necessary.

Self-service. You pump the gas yourself. The self-service price is less than the full service.

Getting a License

You need a state driver's license if you live in the U.S. more than 30 days. You will also use this license as an ID card; you may have to show it when you write a check or apply for credit.

Get a local license at your state's Motor Vehicle Administration (MVA) or Department of Motor Vehicles (DMV). Diplomats and their families should call their embassy or consulate. To get a license, you must be 18–21 years old or older; every state has different laws.

The best time to go is:

- in the morning.
- in the middle of the week.

Mondays and Fridays are busy; so are the first and last few days of a month and the day after a holiday.

 Call and ask what you need to bring. Look under "Motor Vehicle Administration" or "Motor Vehicles-Department of" in the state government section of your phone book. Remember that all documents must be in English or translated, and notarized.

You will probably need:

- an international driver's license or a driver's license from your home country. If you have one, you may not have to take the road test.
- proof of residence. The address must be permanent; you cannot use a hotel address. Bring electricity or telephone bills with your name and address.
- proof of your name and age. Bring an original birth certificate (translated) or other official document—such as your employment authorization card.
- your passport, with your visa and I-94 card.
- Social Security card (see chapter on "When You Arrive"), if you have one.

What if I do not drive? You will need an ID card when you cash a check or apply for credit. If you do not drive, you can get a non-driver's identification card at the MVA or DMV. Bring the documents listed above for getting a license; you will not take any tests.

Words to Know

American Automobile Association (AAA): a club for car drivers. It provides services—such as emergency repairs.

Child safety seat: a car seat for a small child

Department of Motor Vehicles (DMV): (see "Motor Vehicle Administration" below)

Divided highway: a highway with grass, land, or a wall in the middle

Driver education: classes for people who want to learn how to drive and get a license

Driver's manual: a book that tells about driving and parking laws and gives sample driving test questions

Full service: complete gas station service

Gallon: 3.8 liters

Glove compartment: a small storage space in the dashboard of a car

Hazards: flashers; emergency lights on the side and back of a car

Licensed (taxi): allowed by the city or county government to drive a taxi

Meter: a machine in a taxi that tells the cost of the ride; also, a machine on the side of a road. You must put money in the meter to park your car there.

Motor Vehicle Administration (MVA): the state agency in charge of all traffic and auto regulations

Non-driver identification card: an identification card given by the MVA or DMV to people who do not drive

Notarize: to make a document legal; to put an official stamp on a document

Peak hours: (see "Rush hour" below)

Registration card: a card that proves your car is registered by the MVA or DMV

Road test: part of the test you take to get a driver's license. When you take the road test, you drive the car with someone from the MVA sitting beside you.

Rush hour: the time of day when most people are driving to or coming home from work

Seat belts: safety belts attached to the car seats. You must wear seat belts in some states.

Self-service: to pump your own gas

Transfer: a piece of paper that lets you go from bus to bus or from the subway to the bus

Validation: a stamp on your parking ticket that gives you free or discount parking

Fun and Friends

American Holidays

New Year's Day* (January 1): New Year's Eve (December 31). Many Americans have parties on New Year's Eve. They drink a toast to the new year at midnight. Local restaurants and clubs often have special dinner parties. On television, you can see a huge ball drop from a tall building in New York City at exactly 12 am. *Symbol: champagne glass.*

Chinese New Year: Many cities—such as San Francisco—have parades with marching bands, dragon dancers, and clowns. Chinese restaurants often have special meals. *Symbol: Chinese dragon.*

Martin Luther King, Jr. Day* (2nd Monday): Honors the civil rights leader. Ceremonies in all major cities—for example at the Lincoln Memorial in Washington DC, where Dr. King made his famous "I Have a Dream" speech.

Valentine's Day (February 14): Honors the people we love. Children often give cards to family members, teachers, and friends. Often, husbands and wives and lovers give each other gifts—such as candies, cookies, and red roses. *Color: red. Symbol: heart.*

President's Day* (3rd Monday): Honors the birthdays of President Lincoln and President Washington.

Ramadan: A month of fasting, starting in February. Ending with the Eide Al-fetter festival, with food and celebrations in mosques and Islamic centers all over the country.

Black History Month: Special programs in museums and schools celebrate African-American history and culture.

St. Patrick's Day (March 17): Honors an Irish saint. On this day, people of Irish heritage wear green. Cities like New York and Boston have big parades. *Color: green. Symbol: 3-leaf clover.*

Easter (March or April): A Christian, springtime holiday. Most stores are closed. *Colors: purple and yellow. Symbol: Easter bunny, painted eggs.*

Eide Hijja: Holy day when many Muslims make a pilgrimage to Mecca. Festivals and prayers at mosques around the country.

Mother's Day (2nd Sunday): Honors mothers. Children and husbands give cards and gifts to the mothers in the family. Many restaurants have special meals for mothers.

Memorial Day* (last Monday): Honors soldiers killed in war. Many Americans visit soldiers' graves.

 Father's Day (3rd Sunday): Honors fathers. Children and wives give cards and gifts to the father in the family.

 Independence Day* (July 4): Celebrates U.S. independence from England. Cities and towns have parades during the day and fireworks at night. Many Americans have outdoor picnics or barbecues. *Special colors: red, white, and blue. Symbols: the American flag, fireworks.*

 Labor Day* (1st Monday): Honors workers. A weekend of rest when many families go to the beach or the mountains. Outdoor picnics or barbecues are popular.

 Rosh Hashanah and Yom Kippur (end of September or beginning of October): Jewish New Year. Schools and businesses may be closed in cities where many Jews live.

Columbus Day* (2nd Monday): Celebrates the discovery of America.

Symbols: the ships Columbus and his crew sailed on.

Halloween (October 31): "Fun" evening for children. Children wear costumes and go "trick-or-treating"— that is, they visit neighbors' homes and ask for a "treat." Adults often have costume parties. *Colors: black and orange. Symbols: a witch, ghost, or black cat.*

 Veteran's Day* (November 11): Honors U.S. soldiers and the end of World War I. Most big cities have ceremonies; the President often speaks at Arlington National Cemetery in Washington DC.

Thanksgiving Day* (3rd Thursday): Day for giving thanks for all we have. Families eat a big dinner; popular foods are turkey and pumpkin pie. *Symbol: turkey, Indians, Pilgrims (early settlers in Massachusetts who celebrated the first Thanksgiving).*

 Hanukkah (end of December): Jewish holiday that lasts eight days. Many stores, homes, and public places have a menorah. *Symbol: menorah (candlestick with eight branches).*

Christmas* (December 25): Christian holiday. During the holiday season (Thanksgiving to New Year), many Americans give gifts and cards (see "Meeting Americans" chapter). *Colors: red and green. Symbols: Christmas tree, Santa Claus and his reindeer.*

*National holiday. Banks and post offices are closed.

__Dining In & Out__

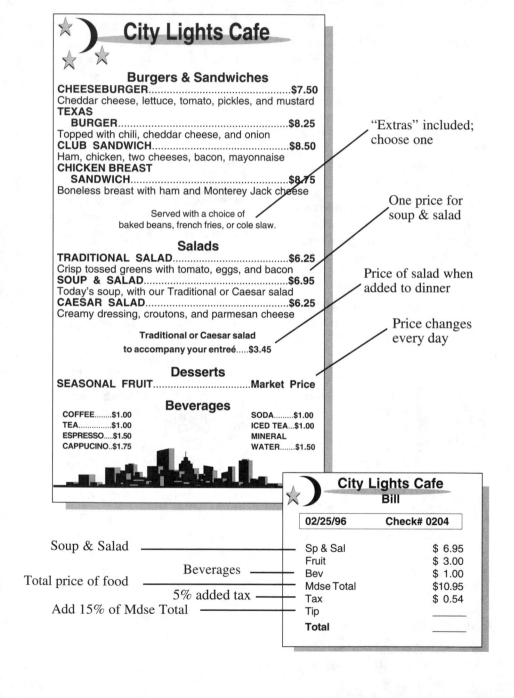

City Lights Cafe

Burgers & Sandwiches
CHEESEBURGER...$7.50
Cheddar cheese, lettuce, tomato, pickles, and mustard
TEXAS BURGER..$8.25
Topped with chili, cheddar cheese, and onion
CLUB SANDWICH..$8.50
Ham, chicken, two cheeses, bacon, mayonnaise
CHICKEN BREAST SANDWICH................................$8.75
Boneless breast with ham and Monterey Jack cheese

Served with a choice of
baked beans, french fries, or cole slaw.

"Extras" included; choose one

Salads
TRADITIONAL SALAD..$6.25
Crisp tossed greens with tomato, eggs, and bacon
SOUP & SALAD...$6.95
Today's soup, with our Traditional or Caesar salad
CAESAR SALAD..$6.25
Creamy dressing, croutons, and parmesan cheese

One price for soup & salad

**Traditional or Caesar salad
to accompany your entreé.....$3.45**

Price of salad when added to dinner

Desserts
SEASONAL FRUIT.................................Market Price

Price changes every day

Beverages
COFFEE........$1.00   SODA.........$1.00
TEA..............$1.00   ICED TEA...$1.00
ESPRESSO.....$1.50   MINERAL
CAPPUCINO..$1.75   WATER.......$1.50

City Lights Cafe
Bill

02/25/96	Check# 0204
Sp & Sal	$ 6.95
Fruit	$ 3.00
Bev	$ 1.00
Mdse Total	$10.95
Tax	$ 0.54
Tip	_____
Total	_____

Soup & Salad

Beverages

Total price of food

5% added tax

Add 15% of Mdse Total

American Foods

Meals

Breakfast. Common breakfast foods are: cereal; toast, bagel, or muffins; eggs; bacon or breakfast sausage; waffles or pancakes; fruit juice; coffee or tea.

Lunch. The most popular time for lunch is 12 or 1 pm. Restaurants serve lunch from 11 am-3 pm. Most Americans eat a light and fast lunch, since lunch breaks last only one hour or less. Common lunch foods are sandwiches, salad, and soup. Lunch menus at restaurants are usually less expensive than dinner menus; but the amount of food you get is less, too.

Dinner. This is the largest meal of the day. In the U.S., people often eat dinner earlier than most Europeans and South Americans—about 6-7 pm. Most restaurants serve dinner from 5–10 pm; restaurants in the suburbs and rural areas may close earlier.

Most dinners include a green salad before the main part of the meal; meat, chicken, or fish; cooked vegetables; and bread.

Some restaurants have "early-bird" specials—usually served around 6–7 pm, depending on the restaurant. The "early-bird" specials are cheaper than the later meals. Usually, you pay one price for a complete dinner.

Brunch. A brunch is one large meal for both breakfast and lunch—most popular on Sundays and holidays, from 11 am–3 pm. Many brunches are buffets; you go up to the food tables and fill your plate as many times as you want.

Restaurants

Many restaurants have menus in the window; you can check the prices and the type of food before you walk in. If a restaurant does not have a menu in the window, go in and ask to see one. It is not impolite to leave after you see the menu.

The prices on the menu do not include tip or tax. Tip waiters about 15%–20% of the bill—before tax. If you did not get good service, you may leave a little less than 15%; but make sure the problem was the *waiter*—and not the kitchen. When you pay, first make sure the tip is not on the bill already; then

To find out about restaurants with foods from your home country, look up "Restaurants" in the Yellow Pages; you may find a list by type of food—for example, French, Chinese, Italian, or Japanese. If you do not eat meat or fish, you can also find "vegetarian" restaurants in this list. To find the names of restaurants with "take-out" or "carryout" menus, look under "Food."

Most bookstores have good restaurant guides—with the names of restaurants, their prices, and menus.

leave the tip on the table or add it to your bill.

The tax will be added to the bill. In most cities, restaurant taxes are 4%–9%.

Types of restaurants

Restaurants (full-service) range from informal to very formal (tie and jacket).

Cafés, coffee shops, and diners serve coffee and pastries, in addition to typical meals.

Cafeterias are self-service restaurants. You take a tray and move through a line, choosing the food you want. Pay at the cash register before you eat. Cafeterias are informal.

Delicatessens (delis) serve sandwiches, salads, and soups. Some have no tables or chairs—you have to take the food with you. Delis are informal.

Snack bars have snacks—such as potato chips, pretzels, and cookies—as well as fast-foods and some sandwiches. Usually there are no chairs—just counters where you can stand while eating. Snack bars are very informal.

Fast-food restaurants serve food that is prepared quickly or made ahead of time—such as hamburgers and french fries. You order "for here" to eat at the restaurant; if you want to take the food somewhere else, order "takeout" or "to go."

Diners also serve food quickly. You can sit at the counter near the kitchen or in a booth. Many diners are open all day and all night; they serve breakfast, lunch, and dinner. The food is simple—for example, for dinner you might get:

- soup
- an entrée such as meat, vegetables, and potatoes
- cake or pie for dessert
- coffee or tea.

Usually, you pay at the cash register when you leave.

Bar restaurants have a bar near the door and tables on the other side of the room; often, you may watch a sports game or see a music video on TV. In some bar restaurants, the bar is bigger than the restaurant; but many fine restaurants also have an open space for drinking.

Young people go to bar restaurants alone or with a friend; but you must be 21 years or older to buy a drink. Bars often have "Happy Hours"—for example, from 5–7 pm. on Friday nights; you can buy drinks at a low price or get hors d'oeuvres for free. Dress is usually business casual or casual (see "Dressing 'Right'" in chapter on "Meeting Americans").

Dinner theaters have food and entertainment—including comedy, musicals, and mysteries. Tickets include entertainment and food, but not drinks, tax, and tip.

Dinner cruises have full-service meals on a boat as it cruises along a river or harbor. Dinner cruises are popular for sightseeing; some dinner cruises have dancing and live music. Tickets include food, but not drinks, tax, and tip.

Dress varies; ask when you buy your ticket.

"Star" restaurants and cafés. Young people all over the world have heard of the "Hard Rock Café" or the "Planet Hollywood." The music is loud and the meals are simple—usually pizza, hot dogs, and hamburgers. You may buy T-shirts and other souvenirs of famous movie or music stars. Dress is casual.

How to dine

1. Call ahead of time.

Make a reservation if the restaurant is very popular—especially on a Friday or Saturday night. Many restaurants do not take reservations. You may need to say if you want "smoking" or "no-smoking" (see below).

Ask about the parking. Is it self- or valet parking? The cost for valet parking is usually $2–$5. If this service is free, tip the driver $1–$2.

2. Arrive no later than 10 minutes after your reserved time.

Give your name when you arrive.

3. Ask for the smoking or non-smoking section.

By law, most restaurants must have a non-smoking area. If you sit there, you cannot smoke. A few restaurants do not allow smoking at all.

Note: It is not impolite to ask for a different table if your table is too noisy or crowded.

4. Order.

Usually, the waiter or waitress will take your drink order first. Water is free; but you may have to ask. Most restaurants offer courses à la carte— you can order the courses separately if you do not want a full-course dinner. Salad is usually offered as a first course.

5. Pay the check (bill).

In some American restaurants, the waiter or waitress gives you the check before you ask for it—sometimes even before you finish eating; you do not have to leave until you want to.

Many Americans share the cost of a meal when they are with friends— that is, they "split the bill," or divide it evenly. At most restaurants, each person in the group may give a credit card and the waiter puts the same amount on each person's bill. If each person wants to pay separately, tell the waiter ahead of time.

6. Ask for a "doggie bag" if you have food left over.

Many restaurants give lots of food; you may want to take some of the food home for another meal or a snack. If you ask for a "doggie bag," the waiter will put the food in a bag or plastic box.

Entertaining At Home

Kinds of parties

Common kinds of parties (see chapter on "Meeting Americans") are:

- **open house.** A few hours when people can come and go as they like (see chapter on "Meeting Americans"). You can serve just drinks and hors d'oeuvres, just dessert, or a buffet meal.
- **dinner party.** Serve "buffet" or "sit-down."
- **cocktail hour.** A few hours when people come and go as they like. Serve drinks and hors d'oeuvres.
- **barbecue.** An outdoor dinner party. Grill the food. Popular foods are hot dogs and hamburgers, chicken, and ribs.
- **"game" party.** A party when people come to watch sports on TV. Serve snacks or a light dinner. Popular foods are pizza, hot dogs and hamburgers, and beer.
- **social get-together**. An evening for conversation, usually starting around 8 pm on a weekend night. Serve hors d'oeuvres, then dessert and coffee or tea.

Invitations

You may:

- phone your guests if you are having just a few people. Tell your guest
  - what time to come (see chapter on "Meeting Americans").
  - what kind of food you are serving. Guests will want to know if you are serving dinner; ask if they cannot eat any foods.
  - what type of clothing to wear (see chapter on "Meeting Americans").
  - how to get to your home.
- mail an invitation. You may include a map showing how to get to your house. You can ask for an R.S.V.P. (a reply) from
  - everyone. Just write your telephone number next to the R.S.V.P. line.
  - only the people who are not coming. Write your telephone number and "R.S.V.P. regrets only."

Saying "thank you"

If you are invited to someone's home, you may want to bring a gift (see chapter on "Meeting Americans"). Call or write to say "thank you" after the party is over.

Caterers

Ready-made. Many gourmet delis, restaurants, hotels, supermarkets, and catering services prepare food platters for parties. You may pick up the food or have it delivered. Buying prepared platters is cheaper than ordering a custom menu or hiring a full catering service. Prices depend on the type and quantity of food ordered.

Prepared in your home. You may hire a caterer to prepare and serve a custom-made menu in your home. Most caterers will also help you plan the menu. Some services provide their own dishes, serving pieces, tablecloths, napkins, and decorations.

Words to Know

À la carte: a menu with a separate price for each item

Bagel: a type of bread. It is round with a hole in the middle. You can get many kinds of bagels—for example, poppy seed, onion, garlic, or "plain."

Brunch: one large meal for breakfast and lunch together

Buffet: a meal where you serve yourself

Cafeteria: a restaurant where you serve yourself and take your food to a table

Cater: to provide food for a party. Caterers cook or bake for you.

Continental breakfast: a breakfast with juice, coffee or tea, and rolls or muffins

Counter: a long table where you sit and eat your food

Course: one part of a meal—for example, the appetizer or dessert

Delicatessen (deli): a restaurant with sandwiches, salads, and soups

"Early-bird" special: a meal served early in the evening—at a lower price

Entrée: main course

Fast-food: food made and served quickly—such as McDonald's hamburgers

"For here": food you eat in the restaurant

Gourmet: special food—usually tastier than ordinary food

Platter: a large plate with meats, cheeses, fruit, or desserts

Reservation: a time when a restaurant saves a table for you

R.S.V.P.: a reply to an invitation. This reply tells whether or not you are coming.

"Sit-down" meal: a meal where the guests sit at a table and the host or hostess serves.

"Take-out": food you get at the restaurant and then take home to eat

"To go": food you take out of the restaurant

Valet parking: personal parking. Someone takes your car when you arrive at the restaurant or party and gets it for you when you leave.

News, Sports, & Entertainment

American Football

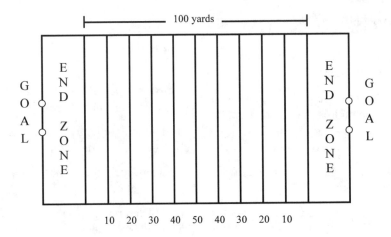

American Baseball

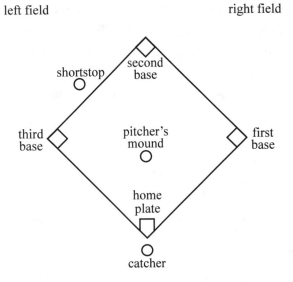

Publications

Your city paper

The city newspaper is the best place to get general information—for example:

- religious events—with lists of religious organizations (see chapter on "Making Friends").
- real estate—with details and advertisements about new homes.
- business and employment sections—advertisements for jobs. This section is more likely to advertise higher-level jobs than the employment section.
- the "arts"—with interviews, reviews, and news about future events.

Newspapers are cheaper if you subscribe, or get home delivery. To subscribe, call the newspaper; look in the Yellow Pages under "Newspapers" and call the number for "Home Delivery." Most major newspapers also publish their news on the Internet.

Other popular dailies

Two daily newspapers read all over the country are:

- *The Wall Street Journal* (business).
- *USA Today* (a popular, easy-to-read newspaper).

Community and ethnic papers

Community newspapers give the news about a local area—for example:

- stores and sales.
- nearby movies.
- clubs and classes (see chapter on "Making Friends").
- jobs—especially jobs for the home, such as home repairs, baby-sitting, and tutoring.

Most community newspapers are published weekly; many are delivered to your home for free. You may also get them at the library or at small food stores in your area.

Most big cities also have foreign language and ethnic newspapers. Look in the Yellow Pages under "Newspapers."

Out-of-town and international papers

You can get these at a few newsstands and bookstores or through the mail. International newspapers cost 75¢–$3 a copy for the daily paper. You can get many of these newspapers on the day of publication, but others (especially international ones) may be 2–3 days late.

Magazines

Most cities have magazines on special subjects such as the theater and the arts. You can also find national magazines on any hobby—for example, travel, autos, hiking, and photography.

Books

Many cities have "living guides" with information on:

- public and private schools for children of all ages.
- best places to shop.
- areas to live in.
- "fun" clubs and organizations (see chapter on "Making Friends").
- sites to see and short trips to take over the weekend.
- activities for children.
- area businesses and kinds of jobs they offer.

Look in the airport bookstore and in local stores. If you use the Internet, you may order some of these books through the Hello! America website (http://www.hellousa.com/world).

Radio & TV

Note: You may be surprised to hear so many advertisements. In some programs, the ads are on every 10 minutes or more.

Public television and radio

The money for public television and radio comes from the government, private businesses, and individuals. The programs on these stations have no advertisements.

AM/FM radio

Your radio has two settings:

- AM. AM stations often have more
  - programs with many advertisements.
  - rock programs.
  - 24-hour news programs.

  - "talk shows" that let people call up, ask questions, and tell what they think.
- FM. Stations on this setting are clearer than most AM stations. Most classical music stations are on FM.

Cable television

This is a paid service that gives you:

- more stations or channels.
- better reception on all channels.

You can find out more about cable TV programs by looking at:

- the special channels on your TV that give program schedules.
- a cable guide—a magazine with all the cable listings. It costs about $1 a month.
- the weekly TV guide in your newspaper or at your local supermarket.

Videos

Renting

Video stores rent VCRs and videos. Most stores have movies (including foreign films), documentary films, exercise programs, and concerts. Some video stores specialize in foreign films.

 You may pay a membership fee in some smaller stores. If you don't return the videotape on time, you pay a "late fee." Most video stores have a "return box" if the store is closed.

Buying

 You may not be able to use the TV set, VCR, CD or audio cassette player from your home country (see chapter on "Before You Come"). Find out what you need for your TV set or any other electronic equipment before you plug it in. Otherwise, you may damage your equipment.

An electronics company that specializes in international electronics can help you choose the attachments or adapters you need. Look in the Yellow Pages under "Sound Systems," "Television," or "Video Recorders." If you need new equipment and plan to return home again, find out what equipment will work in your home country before you buy it.

Most foreign-recorded video and audio cassette tapes cannot be used on American VCRs. You may convert:

- foreign-made cassettes for American machines.
- American-made cassettes for foreign machines.

To have a video converted, call a video production service.

Movies

 Most movie theaters, or cinemas, show each film three or four times a day, especially on weekends. Many movie theaters have 6–8 theaters; you buy tickets for one movie and then leave. If you want to see a popular movie on a weekend night, come early or the movie may be "sold out." Some theaters let you buy the tickets in advance; call and ask. Seats are unreserved.

Many movie houses have special "early-bird" prices—or discounts for shows that start before 6 pm.

Watching Sports

Overview

Baseball, American football, basketball, and ice hockey are the most popular team sports. If you live in a city with a good baseball or football team, many Americans you meet—especially men—will want to talk about the "game." In some cities, football is so popular that you cannot get tickets for any of the "home games" or games played in the team's home city.

You may be able to get a discount for any ticket you buy if you are a:

- student. You must show your ID.
- senior citizen (person over 65).
- child. The age varies.

Ask about discounts when you buy tickets for the movies, concerts or plays, or sports events.

You may watch many professional and college games for these sports on TV.

 You may save money by buying a group of tickets—for example, season or half-season tickets (tickets for all or half the home games). Tickets for college games are usually free for students. If you are not a student, you may buy a ticket; call the college and ask for the "sports information center."

"Game parties." Many fans watch the games every week on TV—often with friends. Pizza and beer are popular at these get-togethers. If you are invited to a "game party," dress casually—for example, wear jeans, a shirt and sweater, and sneakers.

Baseball

Professional baseball starts in April and ends with the World Series in

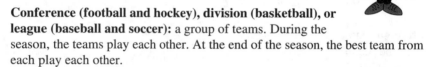

Sports Words

Amateur: a player who does not get money for playing a sport

Cheerleader: a woman or man who marches, dances, and leads songs to cheer on the team

Conference (football and hockey), division (basketball), or league (baseball and soccer): a group of teams. During the season, the teams play each other. At the end of the season, the best team from each play each other.

Defense: the team that does not have the ball or puck, or is not batting. It tries to keep the other team from scoring.

Division: (see "Conference")

Foul: an action that is not allowed and is usually penalized

Goal: place, or area, where hockey or soccer teams score

League: (see "Conference")

Offense: the team with the ball or puck, or that is batting

Pass: to throw or send the ball or puck to another player on the same team

Playoffs: games at the end of the season. The best teams play each other to determine the champion.

Professional: player who is paid a salary for being on a team

Referee or umpire: the person who decides if the players follow the rules

Season tickets: tickets for all the games played in the home city during the season—not including the playoffs

October. Each team belongs to the American League or the National League. During the World Series, the top teams from each league play each other. The team that wins four out of seven games wins the Series.

Football

Professional football has two conferences—the American Conference and the National Conference. The season starts in September and ends with the Superbowl on the last Sunday in January.

Almost all professional players played in college first. The best college teams are picked for different "bowls" such as the Cotton Bowl or Rose Bowl.

Basketball

The professional games begin in October. National Basketball Association (NBA) teams from the four divisions (groups) play a season that lasts until April. Playoffs then continue until the end of June.

The college season starts in November and ends with the National College Athletic Association (NCAA) tournament in March. In the tournament, 64 college teams play for three weeks to see which team will be the champion.

Ice Hockey

The National Hockey League (NHL) has two conferences—with 26 American and Canadian teams.

Professional hockey begins in October and ends with the Stanley Cup in June.

Soccer

Soccer has become more popular in the last few years—especially with young people.

Since 1996, the U.S. has had a professional league with eight teams.

The Arts

Galleries

 Most galleries with art for sale are free. You may come in, look at the art, ask questions—and leave. To get notices of special events and shows in the mail, sign the guest book.

 Most galleries are closed on Mondays.

Museums

 If you plan to visit a museum often, you may pay to be a member. Members enter for free and get information about the museum's activities ahead of time. For example, the Museum of Modern Art in New York City shows movies every weekend; if you wait until the day of the movie, you may not be able to get a ticket.

Most counties and cities have sports teams for children of all ages. Usually, the fathers coach the teams (see chapter on "Older Children").

Some museums are closed on Mondays.

Music and Theater

 In some cities, you may get discounts or tickets for half-price on the day of the show. Call the theater and ask how to buy them. For example, in New York City, the you can get half-price tickets for many shows at Times Square; but you may wait in line a long time.

Libraries

Public Libraries

 Public libraries are free.

What they have. In addition to books and magazines, libraries often have:

- music on records, audio cassettes, and compact discs.
- video cassettes.
- newsletters about topics such as job openings and adult education.
- foreign language books, magazines, and newspapers. Ask which library in your county or city has the language you want.
- reference books—such as encyclopedias and directories in the reference section. You cannot borrow these books; but you may look at them in the library.
- computers you may use for writing, editing, printing, and looking at databases. For example, you may use the computer to get information about
  - all the books in your county or city library system.
  - the stock market.
- activities—such as adult educa-

Football Words

Interception: a play. A player on the offense passes the ball to a team member, but a player on the defense catches it instead.

Fumble: a play. A player for the offense drops the ball and any player on the field can pick it up.

Half-time: the time in between the first and second parts of the game. Usually, the cheerleaders and band from the home team entertain the audience.

Tackle: a play. A player on the defense forces a ball-carrying player on the offense to the ground.

Quarterback: a player on the offense who passes the ball. The quarterback is one of the most important players on the team.

Touchdown: a play that gets the ball to the goal line for six points. Usually, the offense runs with the ball or passes it to get a touchdown.

tion courses and storytelling sessions for children.

To borrow, or take out, books, get a card at the information desk; you must show proof of residence—for example, a utility bill or copy of your lease. Each member of your family may get a separate card.

Rules: Find out:

- how many books or cassettes you can take out.
- how long you can keep these books and cassettes—usually 2–3 weeks for books and 1–7 days for a tape.
- how much you will pay if you do not return the books on time.

Baseball Words

Base: padded objects at three points in the diamond that runners touch as they try to score.

Batter: an offensive player at home plate who tries to hit the pitched ball with a bat

Bleachers: the cheapest seats—usually in the outfield. They do not have a cover or roof overhead.

Catcher: the defensive player who stands behind home plate and catches the ball the pitcher throws

Home plate: the place at the bottom of the diamond where the batter stands and where runners must reach to score

Home run (or homer): A hit (usually out of the ballpark). With a home run, the batter has the time to run all the bases and return to home plate. If any players are on base, they run to home plate too. The team gets one run for each player who gets to home plate.

Infielder: a player on the defensive team who stands near first, second, or third base. Shortstops stand between second and third base.

Inning: a segment of the game. Each game has nine innings. Both teams get a turn at bat during the inning.

Out: a play that prevents the batter from running around the bases. After three outs, the team gives up its chance to score runs and the other team tries to score.

Outfielder: a player who guards the field behind the bases

Pitcher: the player who throws the ball that the batter tries to hit

Run: a point. The team with the most runs after nine innings wins the game.

Umpire: person who decides if the player has followed the rules

- what the hours are.

 Return the books and cassettes before or on the due date; if you are late, you will pay a fee. For example, the late fee for a videotape is $5 a day in some cities. If the library is closed, look for a "Book Drop" slot on the outside wall. In some counties or cities, you may return your books to any library branch within the same county.

 What if I want to keep the book past the due date? Bring the book to the library and say you want to renew it. If you cannot get to the library in time, call and ask if you can renew your book on the phone.

Words to Know

AM radio: a kind of radio station. Most AM stations have rock music and talk shows.

Broadcasts: programs on the radio or TV

Cable television: a paid TV service. You get extra channels and better reception on your TV.

Conversion: changing something (a video cassette or a machine)

Dailies: newspapers published every day

Ethnic: belonging to a certain group of people in the U.S.—such as African-Americans; Asian-Americans; or Latin Americans.

FM radio: a type of radio station. The broadcast is clearer than most AM stations.

Home delivery: a service that brings the newspaper to your door

Public television or radio: a channel or station that gets money from the government, businesses, or individuals. They have fewer advertisements than other channels or stations.

Season tickets: tickets for every home game or performance for the season

Subscribe: to pay for a newspaper or magazine to be delivered regularly to you

Talk shows: a kind of radio or TV program. People call in and ask questions or tell what they think.

Video machine (VCR): a machine to watch videotapes or record TV shows

Meeting Americans

Saying Hello

Marcia: Hello! How are you?
Ahmed: OK. How are you?
Marcia: I met your friend last
night... You know,
the one who is a
writer. I told him I
know you...

Note: Marcia and Ahmed say
"hello" with "How are you?"
They do not tell each other
how they are feeling.

Saying Good-bye

Marcia: Ahmed, I'm late for
an appointment right
now. Can I call you
back? This evening?
Ahmed: Sure. I'll be home.
Marcia: Thanks. Talk to you
then.

Note: Marcia says good-bye
with only a few words.

Saying "Hello"

Names

First and last names. Most Americans use first, or non-family, names when they are meeting for the first time. They also use nicknames—such as Jim for James or Judy for Judith.

Middle names. Some women use their maiden name between their first and last names—such as Carol Smith Taylor.

Mr. and Ms. (pronounced "Miz") To be more formal, Americans use:

- Ms. for married and unmarried women—for example, Ms. Smith. Some women prefer Miss for unmarried women and Mrs. for married women.
- Mr. for married and unmarried men—for example, Mr. Harrison.

Use Mr. or Ms. if you are meeting:

- your boss for the first time.
- someone much older than you.

Sir, Miss, and Ma'am. Use these titles for people you don't know personally—such as a waiter or waitress, mail person, or clerk in a store. "Ma'am" is especially popular in the southeastern part of the U.S. Do not whistle or make loud noises to get someone's attention.

Titles of respect. Use a title of respect for a:

- high college or university official: President Marcus, Professor Smith, or Dean Harrison.
- high government official: Senator Lombardi, Mayor Ferris, or Ambassador Evans. Use "Congressman" or "Congresswoman" for members of the U.S. House of Representatives.
- religious leader: Reverend Samuels, Father O'Connor, or Rabbi Cohen.
- medical doctor or dentist: Dr. Peters.
- person who has earned a doctoral degree: Dr. Halley.

Customs may vary across the U.S.—and even in the same city. Watch the people around you; then you will know what others expect from you.

Remember: You need not act "just like an American" if you do not want to. These chapters tell what Americans expect—*not what you must do.* In general, Americans do not mind if you dress differently or do not speak English perfectly. Other differences may cause problems. These are the differences that Americans may notice—but never talk about with you:

- being on time.
- personal hygiene.
- eye contact.
- personal space.

Body language

Shaking hands and kissing. Shake hands when you are meeting a man or woman for the first time. Women often kiss on one cheek if they are friends—that is, they put their cheeks together and kiss in the air; they often hug each other at the same time. Male friends shake hands or pat each other on the back. Shake hands or kiss again when you say good-bye. A man and a woman may kiss on the cheek if they are friends.

Smiling and eye contact. Americans smile and look each other in the eye when they meet. Look at an American's eyes for just a few seconds when you meet. Look again once in a while you are talking; again, eye contact lasts just a few seconds. In the U.S., eye contact helps people trust each other.

Smiling is also important. Americans smile often—sometimes even at strangers. For example, a stranger may look at you and smile when you are walking on the street or riding the subway. The smile and eye contact are a way of saying "hello"; if you smile back, people may even say "hello" or "hi" as they pass. The smile and the "hi" do not mean the person wants to stop and talk.

Personal space. Americans expect you to stand about two feet (approximately one-half meter) away during the conversation. How can you tell if you are standing too close or too far? If an American keeps stepping backward, you know you are standing too close. If the American keeps stepping forward, you are too far away.

Dressing "Right"

Overview

(See chapter on "Shops & Malls" for a chart on European and American sizes). American dress may vary with:

- the time of day. Get-togethers are often more formal in the evening than in the afternoon.
- people's age. Younger people are more casual than older people. For example, people in their 20s may wear jeans and T-shirts to all social get-togethers.
- the region. People may dress more casually in some regions or cities—for example in areas near San Francisco and San Jose, CA.
- the season. For example, a restaurant may be very casual in the summer—especially if it has outdoor tables; in the winter, you may need more formal clothes.
- the business or corporation. In some offices, men wear a tie and jacket every day; women wear suits (jackets and skirts), pants

Most American buildings have the same temperature all year round—no matter what the weather. In the summer, wear a light jacket or long-sleeved shirt to a restaurant or theater; otherwise, the air conditioning may be too cold for you. In the winter, be ready to take off a heavy sweater; most places are well-heated.

Dressing "Right"

Casual or "sporty"	Shopping malls, sports games, barbecues and picnics, informal restaurants, everyday errands.	Jeans or shorts; T-shirt, long- or short-sleeved sports shirt; sweatshirt; sneakers.	Jeans or shorts; T-shirt, long- or short-sleeved sports shirt; sweatshirt; sneakers.
Business casual	Social get-togethers, most restaurants, many offices. Afternoon plays, ballets, and concerts, all performances for small theaters.	Skirt or long pants, sometimes with a jacket; blouse or sweater; low-heeled or flat shoes.	Long pants; short or long-sleeved shirts; jacket with no tie; shoes (rather than sneakers).
Everyday business	Most offices, dinner parties and dinner at fine restaurants. Evening plays, ballets, and concerts.	Dresses or suits; blouses or sweaters; shoes with low or high heels.	Suit and tie; long-sleeved white or light-colored shirt; shoes.
Formal	Formal cocktail parties and special occasions, such as weddings. Usually the invitations says "black tie" or "formal." Operas at major opera houses, especially at night; opening night is usually fancy.	Fancy dress or suit; low- or high-heeled shoes.	Tuxedo; white shirt and cummerbund; black tie; dress shoes.

Note: Adults and children change their clothes every day. Most have 5-6 outfits or more, so they don't wear the same clothes in one week.

 Women do not wear "topless" bathing suits on most public beaches or at pool parties.

suits (jackets and pants), or dresses. In other offices, men and women wear jeans and loose sweaters. In most cases, people who meet customers or clients usually dress more formally.

If you do not know what to wear to a party, ask:

- your host or hostess when you are invited.
- a salesperson in the clothing store. For example, if you are invited to an evening wedding, ask the salesperson if the dress is "right" before you buy it.

National dress. In most major cities, Americans are used to clothing from other countries and will not stare. You may wear the dress or head covering from your homeland at any social get-together—either casual or formal and in most offices.

Personal Habits

Smoking. Many Americans do not want people around them to smoke. In fact, smoking in public places is often illegal. If you do not see ashtrays around you, ask if you can smoke. Usually, you may not smoke in the rest room.

Look for "smoking-designated areas" in public places such as:

- restaurants. The host or hostess will ask if you want "smoking" or "non-smoking" when you come in. Some restaurants are "smoke-free." If your table does not have an ashtray, ask if you can smoke.
- shopping malls. Many shopping malls are "smoke-free"; look for the "no-smoking" sign at the door to the mall.
- airports. Many airports have smoking sections; but sometimes the whole airport is "smoke-free." If you don't see any ashtrays, do not "light up."
- buses and trains. Look on the window of each car for the "smoking" and "non-smoking" signs.
- office buildings. Most offices are smoke-free; many smokers stand outside the office building and smoke during their break.
- doctors' offices and hospitals. Most do not allow smoking at all—or only in certain places.
- schools and universities. Most have strict rules about smoking.

Alcohol. Wine and beer are popular with dinner or at evening get-togethers.

You must 21 or older to buy any alcoholic drink in a liquor store, supermarket, or bar or nightclub. If you are young, you may need to show an ID that shows your age.

Private homes. Many Americans do not like smoking in their homes; ask. Guests often go outside to smoke; just say "Excuse me. I'm going outside for a cigarette."

All states have strict laws against driving after drinking alcohol. In many states, a policeman can stop you and test your breath; you will pay a fee or even lose your license if you drink and drive.

Personal hygiene. You probably will notice that:

- most Americans bathe or shower every day; in general, they do not like any type of body odor, strong perfumes, or strong after-shave lotions.
- American women usually shave their legs and their underarms.

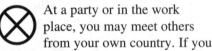 At a party or in the work place, you may meet others from your own country. If you still want to meet Americans, arrange to meet the person from home another time. Do not have a long conversation in your own language.

Being on Time

In general, Americans expect you to come at the exact time. If you:

- know you will be late, call ahead and tell the person you are meeting.
- are already late, say "I'm sorry" and tell why you were not on time.

Social get-togethers

Parties at home.

Do not come more than five minutes early for any party at a home; often, the host or hostess is still getting ready.

In general, if the invitation gives the starting and ending time, you do not need to be on time. For example, if the invitation is from 2–5 pm, you may come at 2:30 or even 2:45 if you like; people often stay about 30 minutes after 5—usually no later.

Dinner parties. Arrive no more than 15 minutes after the exact time; the hostess probably has a meal planned for a certain hour. Do not leave right after the meal is over; wait at least 30 minutes.

Cocktail parties. The invitation will tell you the party hours. Most people do not arrive at the exact time; you may come 30-45 minutes late.

Informal get-togethers. Come no later than 20 minutes after the exact time.

Open house parties. Come any time during the hours on the invitation.

Restaurants. Come no more than 10 minutes early or 10 minutes late. At some restaurants, you will wait—even if you have reservations. Other restaurants will not save your table if you are more than 15 minutes late.

After a party, call up or write a thank-you letter to the host. Your "thank-you" should be short. You may tell the host that the food was good or that the people were "interesting" or "fun to be with."

Appointments. Come at the exact time. Many Americans do not like to wait; in fact, if you are more than 20 minutes late, the person may not wait to meet you.

"Surprise parties." If the invitation says that the party is a surprise, come 10-15 minutes early or right on time. If you must be late, ask the hostess when you should come.

Business situations

Come at the exact time for all meetings—no more than five minutes early or five minutes late. Being on time is especially important for:

- lunchtime meetings or meals. Often, the person has only an hour for lunch.
- job interviews. Be about 10 minutes early.

Cards & Gifts

The "holiday season"

The holiday season starts after Thanksgiving and lasts until New Year's (see chapter on "Holidays"). Many Americans send cards or gifts.

Cards. You may buy sets of cards at the store or order "personalized" cards from a stationery store. Cards to people who do not celebrate Christmas (for example, Jews and Muslims) should say "Happy Holiday"—rather than "Merry Christmas."

If the person is married, address the card to both the husband and wife—

even if you do not know both of them. Mail cards to:

- co-workers you see every day; include secretaries (see "Business giving" below).
- friends who live out of the country. Americans often put in the card
    - a photograph of their family.
    - a note with news about themselves and their family. Some Americans write a long letter, then copy and send it, with a personal note at the bottom.
- friends you see regularly.

Business giving. Each office has different customs. For example, managers may thank their secretaries by:

- giving them a gift.
- taking them out to lunch.
- sending flowers.

Some offices have rules against sending or giving any gifts. Ask.

Holiday tipping. Tip people who service you regularly. Put the tip in a card; the amount depends on how much they have helped you. You may tip:

- people who deliver your newspaper or mail. Put a small tip ($5–$10) in the card. If you have more than one mail person, you do not need to tip.
- door people in your building. Put a tip in the card if the door person has helped you during the year; check with your neighbors to see how much to give. Tips are usually $15–$50.

- hairdressers. If you have a regular hairdresser, you may give a small tip (less than $15) or a small gift.

Gifts. Most gifts are small ($5–$10); many people bake cookies and wrap them with a bow. You may want to give to:

- your child's teacher. The gift is a "thank you"; the teacher will treat your child the same—whether or not you give a gift.
- good friends. Many Americans give a special gift to their two or three "best friends" or to people who have helped them out during the year.

Special occasions

Other holidays (see chapter on "Holidays").

Celebration parties. In general, bring a gift for all celebration parties. It is not impolite to ask what the person "would like." Call the person giving the party or shower. Some parties are:

- wedding and bridal shower. Many couples make a list of the gifts they want; then they "register" the list at a store. Ask if the couple is "registered." Then go to the store with the list and choose something to send (see chapter on "Shops & Malls").
- graduation, confirmation, bar or bat mitzvah. Popular gifts are books and gift certificates at popular book and record stores.
- baby showers, baptisms, christenings, or brises. Many couples "register" for baby showers.

- surprise birthday party. Some parties have "gag gifts"; bring something funny.
- invitation to a new home. Bring a "house gift" when you are going to the new home of a friend—even if it is not for a party.

Home parties. Bring a gift for:

- dinner parties. Popular gifts are bottles of wine or sherry, candies, and flowers. When you are invited, ask: "What can I bring?" Sometimes, the dinner is "potluck"—that is, everyone brings a dish of food.
- cocktail parties. The most popular gift is a bottle of wine, sherry, or other type of liquor.

Words to Know

Baby shower: a party for a woman expecting a new baby, or for her husband

Baptism: a Christian religious ceremony mainly for babies. The ceremony is usually in a church, with a celebration afterward.

Bris: a Jewish celebration for a newborn boy. The boy is circumcised when he is eight days old. The bris usually takes place in the home.

Bar or bat mitzvah: a religious service and celebration for a Jewish boy or girl at age 13

Bridal shower: a party for a woman who is going to be married

Christening: a Christian religious ceremony that includes baptizing and naming a baby

Cocktail party: a party with appetizers and drinks. Usually, many guests are invited.

Dean: a person in charge of a group of students or study programs at a college or university

First name: the name parents give their children—such as Amy, Robert, Gloria, or Mark. Americans say this name first, then the last, or family, name.

"Housewarming" party: a party for someone who has just moved into a new home

Jeans: pants made of thick, blue cloth

Maiden name: a woman's family name. Most women use their husband's family name after they are married. A few women keep their maiden name.

Last name: the family name—such as Smith, Harrison, or Evans. Americans say this name last.

"Potluck" (meal): a get-together for dinner. Everyone brings a dish to share.

Open house: a kind of party. The host or hostess tells you the hours—such as 2–5 pm. You can come any time after 2 or before 5.

"Smoke-free" environment: a restaurant, shop, mall, or office where you cannot smoke

Sneakers: sports, tennis, or running shoes. The bottoms are rubber and the tops are cloth.

Sweatshirt: a loose, thick cotton shirt. The shirt is soft and loose, with a fluffy lining inside. You may wear a sweatshirt for jogging or other sports.

Making Friends

Jack: Greta, it's so good to see you! How are you?

Greta: Fine, thanks. I'm glad to see you, too.

Jack: I wanted you to meet some of my friends... Let me introduce you.

Note: Men and women shake hands. If they are good friends, they may kiss.

Jack: Greta, these are my neighbors, John and Barbara Weedon.

Greta: *(shaking hands)* Pleased to meet you.

Jack: And this is Carl Post. Carl used to live here, but he's moved away.

Greta: *(shaking hands)* Oh, where do you live now?

Jack: *(leaving)* Someone's at the door. Greta, I'll let you introduce yourself to the others...

Note: Jack expects Greta to introduce herself and start a conversation.

Overview

Many Americans move to a new city every few years. Each time they move, they make new friends. To some, a friend is a person you meet socially—even once in a while; for example, people who stop and chat at work may call each other friends.

Often, Americans may seem too busy to make new friends—especially in large cities. Some newcomers say that people smile, look friendly, and say, "Let's get together sometime"; then they walk away. If you want to meet friends, often *you* must be the one to start.

Where To Go

Getting information

Newspapers. In general, you may get the names and numbers of clubs, religious organizations, and classes from:

- the major newspaper in your city (see chapter on "News, Sports, & Entertainment").
- the local newspaper for your town or county. These newspapers usually have the names of community centers, clubs, and classes in your area.
- ethnic newspapers.

The Chamber of Commerce for your town or county. Find the name in the White Pages—for example, "Riverton (or the name of your town) Chamber of Commerce."

The library. Ask the person behind the desk. Also look in the areas near the door.

The Internet (see chapter on "News, Sports, & Entertainment").

The White and Yellow Pages (see chapter on "The Telephone"). Look in the front sections for the names of religious organizations and clubs.

Places to go

Your neighborhood. In some areas, your neighbors may come to say "hello" when you move in. Often, they bring cakes or cookies. In other neighborhoods, no one seems to notice you. They may not be unfriendly—just "busy." If you feel lonely, introduce yourself when you meet your neighbors on the street. Chat awhile; then ask the person to come and visit.

Religious organizations. Churches, synagogues, mosques, and all other religious organizations usually have:

- groups for singles or couples.
- Bible and history classes for adults and children.
- nursery schools and day care centers.

Look in the Yellow Pages under "Churches."

Ethnic organizations. Most large cities have ethnic groups—such as Korean-Americans, Chinese-Americans, Irish-Americans, or Hispanic-Americans. Sometimes the members have been born in the U.S., but their parents or grandparents were immigrants. These organizations may have:

"Fun" Classes and Clubs

4-year or 2-year colleges	Professional and "fun" classes such as music, art, history, cooking, and dancing. Classes about finding a job or the right career are also popular. 2-year colleges may cost less for county residents.	Find "Schools-Academic-Colleges & Universities" in the Yellow Pages.
Public schools	Professional and "fun" classes.	Find "Schools-Academic-Secondary & Elementary" in the Yellow Pages.
County and city recreation departments	Fun classes. Aerobics, nutrition, and arts and crafts are popular. Many recreation departments have adult teams for sports such as softball, basketball, and soccer.	Find the number of the nearest recreation center in the city or county government section of your phone book under "Recreation."
Libraries	"Book discussion groups" that meet to talk about a different book each month. These may be free.	Find the number of the nearest library in the city or county government section of your phone book under "Libraries."
Community centers	Aerobics and other fun classes. Book discussion groups. Some communities have "welcome clubs" for newcomers; most clubs meet about once a month.	Call the Chamber of Commerce for the names of community centers in your city or county.

 Check to see if you are a resident in your county. For example, in some counties you are a resident if you have paid county property taxes in the past year.

"Fun" Classes and Clubs (cont.)

Young Men's Christian Association (YMCA)	Water sports, basketball, aerobics, fun classes, and clubs. You do not have to be a Christian or a male to join. Usually, you pay an initiation fee and monthly dues.	
Women's centers	Classes and discussions—particularly about choosing the right career, getting a job, and improving professional skills.	Call the Chamber of Commerce or look under "Women" and "Career" in the Yellow Pages.
Health clubs/ fitness centers	Aerobic classes, exercise programs and equipment, swimming. Usually, you pay an initiation fee and monthly dues.	Find "Health Clubs" in the Yellow Pages.
Outdoor clubs	Bird-watching, hiking, biking, or camping.	Ask at a good sporting goods store or find "Clubs" in the Yellow Pages.
Tennis clubs	Group tennis lessons, indoor and outdoor tennis courts for rent. Public courts cost less than private clubs.	Find "Tennis Courts-Public" and "Tennis Courts-Private" in the Yellow Pages.
Country and golf clubs	Social get-togethers, golf courses and lessons. Often, a member must invite you to join a private club; some clubs have a waiting list. The initiation fee may be thousands of dollars. Usually, you also pay annual dues. Public courses cost much less.	Find "Golf Courses-Public" and "Golf Courses-Private" in the Yellow Pages.

To join some health clubs, you must sign a contract. Read the contract carefully; have someone translate if you do not understand it. If you sign a 2-year contract, you will have to keep paying, even if you move out of the area. Most clubs will give you a 6-month contract if you ask.

With many health clubs, you may negotiate the price and terms of the contract.

- social get-togethers—such as picnics and parties.
- business networking groups (see chapter on "Finding a Job").
- schools where children learn language and history on Saturdays or Sundays.
- nursery schools and day care.
- volunteer work to help the poor.

National Council for International Visitors (NCIV). The NCIV has programs in over 100 U.S. cities; with some local programs, you may pay a fee. Most of NCIV's funding comes from the government. If you are still in your home country, call the U.S. Embassy, or the national NCIV number (see "Chapter Information" in the Appendix). If you are in the U.S., call the national number to find out if the NCIV has a local program in your area.

Professional associations. All professions have an association. Many have local chapters; almost all have national and state meetings at least once a year (see chapter on "Finding Work"). Look up the name and number under "Associations" in the Yellow Pages.

Volunteer work. Americans often volunteer, or work for free, in their extra time. Women who do not work often volunteer more than men; but many people with jobs volunteer in the evenings or on the weekends. Some volunteer work may help your career (see chapter on "Finding Work"); but volunteering is also a good way to meet others who have the same interests. Some suggestions are:

- the Parent-Teacher Asssociation (PTA) or other parent organizations. If you have children in school, the PTA gives you the chance to meet other parents and find out more about your child's school. The general PTA meetings are large, and you may not meet anyone. Volunteer to help
  – raise money. For example, many schools have fairs to

The National Council for International Visitors (NCIV) helps international visitors meet Americans with the same professional interests. For example, if you are a teacher, they may be able to find an American teacher to meet with you and talk about American schools; sometimes, you may stay in the American's home for 2-3 days or a week. Other NCIV services are:

- arranging professional meetings and seminars.
- giving out information, maps, and advice.
- reserving hotel rooms.
- help with translations or interpretations.

Every year, the NCIV sponsors about 25,000 international visitors—for example, high government officials, teachers, journalists, business persons, artists, and technicians. Many are students and participants in USIA or USAID programs.

raise money for extra equipment or field trips.
- teach or supervise the children in the classroom, computer lab, or library.
- churches and other religious organizations. You may teach a class, visit the sick, raise money, or deliver food to the poor.
- museums. For example, you may take classes and learn about art, then guide visitors through the museum. Many museums have research programs that use volunteers.
- libraries. For example, you may help put books away or read to children.
- hospitals, old-age homes, and child-development centers.

International student organizations (see "Chapter Information"—"Colleges and Universities"—in the Appendix).

Newspaper "dating" ads. Many newspapers have ads for singles who want to date; the people in the ads tell a little about themselves—their hobbies, age, and gender (male/female), religion, or race. Usually—but not always—the male pays for any food or entertainment; with a "Dutch Treat" date, each person pays his or her own bill.

Dating services. A dating service will match you up with someone for a fee. Be sure you know the cost of the service before you begin.

 Ask other singles about the ads in this newspaper. Women should meet their date

in a public place; do not go home with your date the first or second time. Be sure you know the person and his friends well before you are alone.

Bars and nightclubs. Many singles go to bars and nightclubs on Friday or Saturday nights. Usually, they go with a friend. Some restaurants have "happy hours" when you may buy drinks at a discount or get free hors d'oeuvres.

 If you want to go into a bar or nightclub to meet someone:

- check with someone you know ahead of time; be sure it is safe.
- do not give anyone your address or telephone number; get to know that person first.
- do not go home with anyone alone. If you want to meet someone again, choose a public place with lots of people.

Words to Know

Aerobics: activities and exercises that take a lot of energy

Chamber of Commerce: an organization of businesses. Most counties, cities, and states have a Chamber of Commerce. The U.S. Chamber of Commerce is for the whole country.

Community center: a public club house for the town or village. Usually, you can take classes or join clubs there.

Country club: a club where members can get together socially. Most have a dining room and sports facilities—such as a golf course, swimming pool, and racquetball or tennis courts. Usually, you join for the year.

Ethnic group: group of Americans with families from a different country or area of the world—such as Korean-Americans, Chinese-Americans, Irish-Americans, or Hispanic-Americans

Fitness center: (see "Health Club" below)

Health club: a place to go for exercise, swimming, and fitness classes

Initiation fee: a one-time payment to join a club

Mosque: a place where Muslims pray and celebrate their holidays

National Council for International Visitors (NCIV): an organization that helps international visitors meet or stay with Americans who have the same profession

Parent-Teacher Association (PTA): an organization for the teachers and parents of children in a school

Recreation department: a program with sports, arts and crafts, music, and other classes. Usually, the county or city runs the program. Some programs are only for children; others are for adults and children.

Synagogue: a place where Jews pray and celebrate their holidays

Volunteer work: work you do for free to help a person or an organization. Volunteer work is a good way to help others, improve your jobs skills, or meet others.

Welcome club: a club for people who are new in the area. Most clubs meet once a month.

White Pages: the telephone book that lists people's names, addresses, and home numbers

Yellow Pages: the telephone book that has advertisements for products and services and the phone numbers of businesses. You look up the name of a product or service to find out where to buy it

Young Men's Christian Association (YMCA): an organization with sports, classes, and clubs. You do not have to be a male or a Christian to join. YMCAs are often cheaper than other clubs.

When You Get Here

Food Shopping

Brand name

Average amount used at one time

1/2 less fat
1/3 less calories than similar product

Pepe's Spicy Tomato Soup

Lite

Ingredients:
Water, Diced Tomatoes, Onions, Peppers, Apple Cider Vinegar, Cilantro, Garlic, Herbs and Spices.

Serving size .... 1 Cup
Servings per jar 1

Nutrition Facts

Calories 210	Calories from Fat 15

% Daily Value*

Sodium 60 mg	
Total Fat 1.5g	**2%**
Saturated Fat 0g	**0%**
Cholesterol 0mg	**0%**
Total Carbohydrate 49g	**16%**
Dietary Fiber 8g	**32%**
Sugars 7g	
Protein 9g	

Net Wt. 15½ oz. (439 g.)

may lead to heart disease

may lead to heart disease

salt; may lead to high blood pressure

*Daily values are based on a 2,000 calorie diet.

__Oven Temperatures__

Heat	Fahrenheit	Centigrade	British
Very low	100-250°	40-120°	Regulo 1-5
Low	300°	150°	Regulo 6
Moderate	325-350°	165-180°	Regulo 6-7
Hot	400°	205°	Regulo 8
Very hot	450-500°	235-260°	Regulo 9-10

Note: Most recipes assume that the oven has been *preheated* to the indicated temperature *before* the food is placed in the oven.

Allow about 15 minutes for the oven to preheat before you put the food inside. If you like, you may buy an oven thermometer to be sure your temperature control is accurate.

You may also buy a *meat thermometer,* which shows the temperature inside the meat, so you can tell when it is ready.

Note: The climate and altitude may affect your cooking. For example, in Miami, the humidity makes baking bread or pie crust difficult. In Denver, the high altitude affects the temperature you need for cooking; in this city, you need to keep the oven about 25° hotter than it says in the recipe.

The Supermarket

 If you have the time, visit a few stores before you need to buy anything.

Most supermarkets are open seven days a week. On Mondays through Saturdays, they are usually open from 6 am–11 pm; on Sundays, they close in the early evening. Some supermarkets are open 24 hours every day. The hours should be posted on the door.

Most grocery stores close early or all day on Thanksgiving, Christmas, New Year's Day, and other major holidays.

How to shop

1. Find what you need.

Use a cart or a small basket to carry your food. Above the aisles, or rows, are the names of the items in that aisle. Also, your shopping cart may have a small chart under the handle.

2. Get your check approved.

Go to the manager's office. The manager will sign your check. Fill out an application for a courtesy card (see "Special Services" below).

3. Go to the checkout counter.

If you are buying only a few items, look for the "express lane." With some express lanes, you must pay cash; with others, you may pay with a check or credit card. In most

stores, you can find a lane with "No Candy" near the cash register; look for the sign at the top.

4. The checkout worker scans each item.

The price also comes up on a screen above the cash register.

5. Give the checkout worker your coupons.

The checkout worker subtracts the value of the coupons from your total price.

6. Pay the cashier.

Many major supermarkets accept cash, checks, debit cards, and credit cards. Most also have bank machines where you can use your Automatic Teller Machine (ATM) card.

7. Take your cart to the car or leave it near the door.

In some areas, the bagger takes the cart to your car. In other areas, you may leave your bags in the cart and drive back to pick them up.

? *What if I don't have enough money at the register?* Most stores take a credit card. If you have a bank card, look for an ATM machine.

? *What if I want to return something the next day?* The large supermarkets let you return most items if they are spoiled or if you have changed your mind. Do not return fresh items such as eggs or milk. Take the item and the sales slip to the manager.

What you can find

Produce. Most fresh fruits and vegetables are sold by the pound. They may come packaged or loose. At the checkout counter, the worker weighs and prices the food.

Meat. The meat counter has fresh or frozen:

- beef.
- chicken and other poultry.

Meats are usually graded.

- Prime meat is the best quality and the most expensive. It has more fat and is more tender.
- Choice meat is the most common grade. It has less fat and is less tender.
- Select, or lean, meat is trimmed of fat. It can be tougher than other cuts, but most major supermarkets tenderize the meat.
- Ungraded meats can still be good, but they are usually cheaper and less tender.

To get help, ring the bell near the butcher's window. You may ask the butcher for a special cut of meat or for a package weighing exactly as much as you want (see "Special Services" below).

Poultry. Chicken, Cornish hens, turkey, and other poultry are usually graded AA or A. The most expensive is AA. It has less fat and is the freshest and most tender.

Seafood. The seafood counter has both fresh, frozen, and "previously frozen" seafood. Some common kinds of fish are grouper, salmon, swordfish, flounder, halibut, catfish, and tuna. Common kinds of shellfish are shrimp, clams, mussels, and oysters.

Certain kinds of fish are popular in areas where they can be found. For example, salmon is popular in Seattle; grouper is popular in Miami. In general, though, you will find fish from all over the world.

Dairy products. The dairy case has eggs, milk, cheese, yogurt, and fruit juices. You may also find pickles, sauces, dips, and fresh pasta.

Butter comes by the pound or the stick (¼ lb.). Eggs come in cartons of six (½ dozen) or twelve (1 dozen). The price depends on the size and the grade. The grades are:

- A: good for all kinds of cooking and baking.
- B: mostly used for baking.

Check the dates before you buy.

Delicatessen. The deli counter has fresh salads, hot barbecued chicken, appetizers, and other kinds of prepared

Check the date on the package of fresh food. This shows the last day on which the product can be sold, but you can use it for up to a week afterward.

or cooked foods. Order about ¼ pound (lb.) of meat or salad per person.

It is not impolite to ask the employee to show you food; you may ask him or her to "add a few slices" or "take away a few spoonfuls" or for "a taste" if you like.

Bakery. Baked goods are usually made every day. Sometimes you may buy "day-old" breads or pastries for half-price. If your area has a wet climate, be sure the bread is wrapped tightly so it stays fresh.

You may need to take a number at the bakery or delicatessen counter. The number shows when it is your turn to be waited on.

Frozen foods. These include frozen vegetables, juices, ice cream, meats, fish, breads, and desserts. Frozen prepared meals, such as lasagna, burritos, or TV dinners.

Special diet foods. By law, foods with labels such as "low-fat" or "low-sodium" must meet guidelines set by the federal government.

Baby items. These include strained foods, baby cereal mixes, infant formulas, and even diapers.

Ethnic foods. You can find foods from other countries or cultures—including Oriental, Italian, Hispanic, and kosher canned goods.

Food Labels

By law, the labels on food must mean what they say. For example:

Key Words	What they mean
Fat Free	Less than .5 gram of fat per serving
Low Fat	3 grams of fat (or less) per serving
Lean	Less than 10 grams of fat, 4 grams of saturated fat, and 95 milligrams of cholesterol
Light (Lite)	Less than 1/3 the calories or no more than ½ the fat of similar products; or no more than ½ the sodium of similar versions
Cholesterol Free	Less than 2 milligrams of cholesterol and 2 grams (or less) of saturated fat per serving

To make health claims about...	The food must be...
Heart Disease	Low in fat, saturated fat, and cholesterol
Blood Pressure	Low in sodium

Baking goods. These include ingredients for baking or cooking—such as sugar, flour, and spices. You can also find "mixes" for breads, cakes, cookies, and puddings.

Food bar. You choose hot and cold foods and pay by the pound. The prices are posted for such items as:

- the hot food bar, with cooked meats, chicken, pasta, soups, and chili.
- the cold salad bar, with mostly fresh vegetables and fruits; sometimes it has tuna or egg salad.
- the frozen yogurt machine; the yogurt often comes in two different flavors every day.

Take as much food as you want. The cashier at the counter weighs and prices the food.

Pharmacy. This section has over-the-counter and prescription medicines. You may also find products such as toothbrushes, sanitary napkins, sunglasses, combs and brushes, and shaving lotion.

Photo center. You may buy film or have color photos developed here.

Figuring the Price

Labels. Look for the store's own label. These products often cost less and may be just as good as the food with more famous labels that are sold in many different stores.

Item price. The item price is the price of the package. If two boxes have the same amount of food, you can calculate quickly which brand is cheaper. If not, check the unit price.

Unit price. If two products are the same size, the unit price helps you calculate which product is cheaper. For example, a unit price may show the price per ounce. You may use it to compare two cans of soup—one large and one small; look for this price on the shelf just below the item.

Coupons. Cut these out of the "Food" section of the newspaper or out of magazines or advertisements that come in the mail. Coupons give you a discount on a specific item. Often, you cannot use the coupons:

- after the expiration date printed on the coupon.
- in all stores. For example, they may be good only in the store where you got the coupon.

Sometimes a store has "double" and "triple" coupons (two or three times the value of the coupon). For example, if you have a coupon for 25¢ off Kleenex tissues and it is a double coupon, you will get a 50¢ discount.

Sales tax. Items that are taxed have a "T" after them on the sales slip. In general, basic foods such as meat, milk, bread, and produce are not taxed.

Large supermarkets usually have rest rooms at the back of the store. Ask an employee where they are.

Snack foods and some household items are taxed in some areas.

Special Services

Special orders. Most stores take advance orders for meat, fish, or pastries. For example, you can order a turkey or ham about a week before Thanksgiving or Christmas. If you are having guests, you may order special cuts of meat, deli platters, or desserts.

Repackaging. You may buy a smaller slice of watermelon or a smaller piece of fish; ask.

Coffee. Many grocery stores grind fresh coffee beans for you to take home. Some have coffee grinders next to the coffee beans so you can grind the coffee yourself.

Home delivery. Some stores offer home delivery. You can give your order over the telephone and have the groceries delivered to your house on the same day. You may have to pay for this service.

Check cashing. The courtesy or check-cashing card lets you cash a check easily. The card is good at all stores with the same name. If you need money, some large supermarkets also let you write a check for $20–$50 more than the amount of the bill; you get the money back in cash.

To get a courtesy card, go to the manager's office and ask for an application. If you have a bank account in the area, you should get a card in the mail within a few weeks. Some stores give temporary cards.

Specialty Stores

Natural Foods

Many supermarkets carry natural, or organic, foods—that is, foods with no chemicals. You can also find natural food stores in many communities.

Ethnic Grocers

Every large city has ethnic grocery stores where you can meet people from your home country and get the kinds of foods you like. You may find videotapes, audiotapes, books, and newspapers in your own language.

Look under "Grocers—Retail" in the Yellow Pages. Also look in the Business Section of the White Pages for business names that start with the name of your country.

Words To Know

Altitude: height, or number of feet, above sea level. If your area is high above sea level, you may need to change the way you cook.

Brand name: the name of the company on the label

Checkout counter: where you go to pay for items

Choice: the most common grade of meat

Coupon: a piece of paper that gives a discount on the price of a specific item

Courtesy or check-cashing card: a card that lets you pay with a check

Dairy products: products made from milk—such as milk, cheese, or yogurt

Debit card: a bank card used to pay for something. The money is taken out of your account right away.

Deli platter: a large plate with meats and cheeses, and sometimes salads

Express lane: "fast lane"; lane for shoppers who have only a few items

Graded: a way of telling how good a product is. For example, meat is graded prime, choice, or lean.

Home delivery: a service that sends the groceries to your home

Humidity: wetness in the air. The humidity may affect the way you bake.

Item price: what one box or package costs

Lean: a type of meat with very little fat

Natural foods: foods grown or made without chemicals

Organic foods: natural foods—with no chemicals

Prime: the best and most expensive cut of meat

Produce: fresh fruit and vegetables

Repackaging: to pack again; putting less or more food in a package

Sales slip: a paper that lists what you bought and how much it costs

Sales tax: the value-added tax. Meat, milk, bread, and produce are not taxed. Snack foods, such as potato chips, are taxed.

Scan: to put an item in a certain place so the machine can read the price

Select: a type of meat with very little fat; lean

Special order: an order for meat, fish, or pastry that the store will make for you—for example, deli platters or fresh whole poultry

TV dinner: a frozen meal that comes in a tray

Unit price: the price for each unit of measure—usually pounds or ounces

Ungraded: a cheaper and less tender type of meat

Shops & Malls

"Misses" Dresses, Coats & Skirts

American	3	5	7	9	11	12	13	14	15	16	18
European	36	38	38	40	40	42	42	44	44	46	48
British	8	10	11	12	13	14	15	16	17	18	20

Sweaters & Blouses

American	10	12	14	16	18	20
European	38	40	42	44	46	48
British	32	34	36	38	40	42

"Junior Miss" Dresses or Suits

American	3	5	7	9	11	13	15
European				34	36	38	40

Shoes

American	5	6	7	8	9	10
European	36	37	38	39	40	41
British	3½	4½	5½	6½	7½	8½

Suits, Overcoats and Sweaters

American	34	36	38	40	42	44	46	48
European	44	46	48	50	52	54	56	58
British	34	36	38	40	42	44	46	48

Shirts (Come in combination of neck and sleeve sizes [32-36])

American	14½	15	15½	16	16½	17	17½	18
European	37	38	39	41	42	43	44	45
British	14½	15	15½	16	16½	17	17½	18

Shoes

American	7	8	9	10	11	12	13
European	39½	41	42	43	44½	46	47
British	5½	6½	7½	8½	9½	10½	12½

Measurements

American & Metric Systems

	American	Metric
Length	1 inch (1")	2.54 centimeters
	1 foot (1')	0.305 meter
	1 yard	0.914 meter
	1 mile	1.609 kilometers
Area	1 square inch	6.452 sq. cm.
	1 square foot	929.030 sq. cm.
	1 square yard	0.836 sq. m.
	1 acre	4,047 sq. m.
Volume/Capacity		
	1 pint	0.473 liter
	1 quart	0.946 liter
	1 gallon	3.785 liters
Weight	1 ounce	28.350 grams
	1 pound	453.592 grams
	1 ton	0.907 metric ton

	Metric	American
Length	1 centimeter	0.394 inch
	1 decimeter	03.937 inches
	1 meter	39.37 inches
	1 kilometer	0.621 mile
Area	1 square cm.	0.155 sq. in.
	1 centare	10.764 sq. ft.
	1 hectare	2.477 acres
Volume/Capacity		
	1 deciliter	0.211 pint
	1 liter	1.057 quarts
	1 decaliter	2.642 gallons
Weight	1 decagram	0.353 ounce
	1 kilogram	2.205 pounds
	1 metric ton	1.102 tons

Overview

Comparing

Americans are used to "shopping around"; that is, they compare before they buy. Many newcomers are surprised by the big difference in:

- the prices of the items.
- the quality of the items, or how good they are.
- the services different stores offer.

When you "shop around," it is not impolite to talk about the item with a sales clerk for a while and then say you want to think about it.

Paying

How to pay. Most stores expect you to pay with a check or credit card; if you pay with a check, you usually need two forms of identification (ID):

- a photo ID—such as a driver's license or employee ID.
- a credit card.

Adding up the cost. Most states and cities have a sales tax. This tax is like a VAT (value-added tax); but it is added to the price you see. The tax is a percentage of the price. For example, with a 6% sales tax, you will pay $10.60 for an item listed at $10.

⊗ Be careful when paying with a credit card. Anyone who knows the information on your card can call a mail-order company and charge an order to you. If you get a carbon paper (black paper) in between the copies of the receipt, tear it up.

Returning and exchanging

Sales slips. Always save sales slips. Most stores will return your money if you are unhappy with a product. Some require that you return it in a specific time period—for example, within two weeks.

Many small stores offer "store credit only" for returns—that is, you can get something else in the store for the same or greater price; but you will not get your money back.

Returning items. Go to the department where you bought the item. Ask to see a salesperson; if possible, have the product and the sales slip with you. Explain why you are unhappy with the product.

Note: You do not need a "good" reason for returning most items. Just say you changed your mind.

 What if I buy something that is not good and the management will not refund my money? Contact the Office of Consumer Affairs in the city or county where the purchase was made. It will tell you what to do. Find the number for "Consumer Affairs" in your county or city government section of the telephone book.

Shopping Malls

 Mall hours are different in each region; but the hours usually are:

- during the week, 10 am–9:30 pm.

- Saturdays, 10 am–5 or 6 pm.
- Sundays, 12 pm–5 or 6 pm.

Around Christmas time, most malls are open from 9 am–9 pm.

Stores and services

Stores. Most malls have:

- specialty stores, or stores specializing in books, electronics, furs, shoes, gifts, clothing, toys, jewelry, sporting goods—and anything else you can name!
- department stores, or large stores with many kinds of items. You may buy linens, jewelry, shoes, pajamas, TVs, and stationery. Many department stores also have beauty salons and photography services.

Directories. Usually, you can find store directories where the main hallways come together. You may also ask at the information desk.

Rest rooms. Every mall has at least one public rest room on each floor, especially near the food court. Department stores also have rest rooms.

Restaurants. Most malls have food courts, or large areas with tables and many types of foods. The food is served "over-the-counter," or cafeteria style. Food courts are usually less expensive than more formal restaurants. They are also good for families, because everyone can get a different kind of food. You may also find more formal restaurants around the mall or in some department stores.

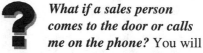

What if a sales person comes to the door or calls me on the phone? You will get many sales calls on the phone—especially around 7 or 8 pm. A few salespeople will come to your door in the middle of the day. *Remember*—it's your money! You do not have to buy anything. Just close the door or hang up the phone if you like.

Special Services

Alterations

Many stores do alterations, or tailoring, if necessary. The service is convenient; but the cost is usually higher than the cost of tailoring from a dry cleaning shop.

Personal shoppers

Some department stores have personal shoppers. This service is free for items bought in that store. Personal shoppers can help you:

- choose gifts.
- buy clothes.
- decide what to wear for different occasions.
- choose makeup and hair styling.

Some personal shoppers even bring items to your home; find out if they charge you for the visit. If you find a personal shopper you like, you may call ahead of time and make an appointment.

Home decorators

Like personal shoppers, home decorators give personal attention. You may use department store decorators for free. Often, they come to your home and give advice on furniture, carpets, drapes, and wallpaper. Private decorators may charge by the hour or by the amount you buy.

Special orders

Sometimes, a store may not have the exact item you need. Ask if the store can place a special order.

Shipping

Many stores will ship an item anywhere in the U.S. for a small fee. This service is convenient for sending gifts out of town. If you like, someone may gift-wrap the present for you; then you may attach a card and send it—all from the store where you bought it.

Gifts

Gift wrapping. Usually, the store gives you a free box if you ask. Many stores gift-wrap for a fee; some stores have cards to put inside the box.

Gift certificates. Gift certificates are common for graduations, birthdays, and Mother's or Father's Day. For example, a person who has a $50 gift certificate can spend $50 in that store. You may buy gift certificates at many kinds of stores—such as department stores, record stores, and small specialty shops.

Bridal registry. Brides often register at a store to help people choose gifts. The bride and groom make a list of the items they want and give the list to a store. When you go to the store, the salesperson looks up the name of the couple and shows you the items on their list. The store also keeps track of the items that have been bought already.

If you have a credit card, you can buy and send the gift over the telephone. You may choose the gift, charge it, and have it mailed—without ever leaving your house! You pay with a credit card.

Baby registry. The baby registry is like the bridal registry (see "Bridal registry" above). Ask for the children's department.

Catalogs

Advantages

Catalogs allow shoppers to buy items from their home.

You may get catalogs in:

- large department stores.
- the mail. Often catalogs come in the mail even if you have not asked for them.

With catalog shopping, you get:

- a wide choice. You have more colors and sizes to choose from.
- convenience. You may order from most catalogs by phone, seven days a week, night or day. Most catalogs mail outside of the U.S. Many catalogs also take

orders—with a credit card or check in U.S. dollars—from foreign countries.

The disadvantages are:

- cost of returns. If you return the item, you usually will not get back the cost of sending it to you. Also, you will pay postage to send the product back.
- delivery delays. The company may not have what you ordered. Sometimes the delay is only a few days, but it may be a month or more.

How to order

To order by mail, cut the order form from the catalog, fill it out, and mail or fax it to the catalog company. The company will need the number of your credit card and the expiration date on the form or a check. You may use the telephone to order if you have a credit card.

 The delivery cost is usually a percentage of the cost of the item; add this to the price. You may or may not pay a sales tax— depending on the location of the store.

Bargain Hunting

 In general, do not bargain in stores—even when items are on sale. Often, you may bargain if you are buying from individual sellers.

Advertisements

Classifieds. The classified ads in the back of the newspaper are mostly from people who want to sell something secondhand (used).

Store ads. Stores often advertise sale items in newspapers. If you see an item that interests you, call the store to find out more about it. Make sure you know when the sale ends and if there are any restrictions, or circumstances when the sale price is not good.

Special sales

When you go to a store for a sale item, take the ad with you. If the store has no more of that item, a dealer will sometimes give you a "rain check"; that is, you may buy the item at the same sale price at a later time.

It is not impolite to ask the salesperson if an item will go on sale soon.

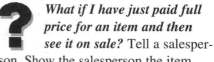 *What if I have just paid full price for an item and then see it on sale?* Tell a salesperson. Show the salesperson the item and your receipt; you usually get the discount.

Discount shopping

Discount stores have lower prices. There are discount stores for almost every kind of item. Pay special attention to the return policies; sometimes there are no refunds.

Warehouse clubs are huge stores that sell name-brand products at lower prices. The prices are cheaper— sometimes almost half those in the regular stores. About 25% of the items in a warehouse club are food products that are frozen, canned, and boxed; most warehouse clubs do not have fresh food. Also, you may have to buy "in bulk"—for example, three detergent boxes instead of one. Warehouse clubs also have office supplies, small appliances, sporting equipment, household products, clothes, and many other kinds of products.

To shop in a warehouse club, you usually must:

- pay a membership fee—around $35.
- meet certain standards set by the club. If you work for a large company, you probably will meet these standards.

Discount stores are smaller than warehouse clubs; their prices may not be as low, but you do not have to buy in bulk or pay a membership fee. You can find discount stores for almost anything—including clothing, furniture, leather goods, shoes, and sporting equipment. Look at the ads in the newspaper to find the discount store you want.

Outlet malls get their products right from the factory and sell them for a lower price. Ask if the item is a "second," or slightly damaged; if it is, look closely to see what could be wrong. For example, look for stains, missing buttons, loose threads, and holes.

Garage/yard sales are usually in private homes. Most items for sale are used. You may find antiques, old books, furniture, clothes, or dishes.

You cannot return what you buy, but you can bargain.

Consignment shops sell used items, such as clothing, home lamps, or books. You cannot return what you bought. Usually, you cannot bargain.

Flea markets are public markets with many kinds of items. Most flea markets are outdoors, but some larger ones are indoors.

Flea markets usually sell used items— such as furniture, clothes, jewelry, and antiques. As with yard sales, you cannot return items, but you can bargain.

Words to Know

Alteration: the changing of clothes so they fit you

Baby registry: a list of gifts that parents want for their baby

Bridal registry: a list of gifts for the bride and groom

Bulk: (items) in large quantities. Usually, you get a discount for buying "in bulk."

Cafeteria: a restaurant where you serve yourself and bring the food to a table

Catalog: a book that shows pictures and tells about the items for sale. You can call or mail in your order.

Classified section: a section of the newspaper that lists items for sale

Consignment shop: a store that sells used items

Discount store: a store that sells items at lower prices

Flea market: an open area where people sell items on tables or in tents. Flea markets are good for items such as antiques, furniture, jewelry, audio and video cassettes, clothing such as jackets and hats.

Food court: an area in a mall or shopping center with many types of fast-food restaurants

Garage/yard sale: sales in private homes. Usually items for sale are used.

Gift certificate: a kind of gift. To buy someone a gift certificate, go into the store and pay for the certificate at the cash register. When you give the certificate to your friend, he or she can use it to buy something at the store.

Gift wrap: to cover a package with pretty paper and a bow

Mail-order company: a company that sends you products in the mail. You order by calling or sending a check.

Mall: a shopping area in one building with many kinds of stores

Name-brand product: a product made by a major company

Outlet mall: a mall with discount stores

Personal shopper: a person who helps you choose gifts and buy clothes

Rain check: a paper that lets you buy an item for a lower price after the sale is over

Receipt: a paper you get from the store when you buy something which shows the items purchased and the amount paid

Refund: to return money

Sales taxes: the taxes you pay when you buy something

Sales slip: (see "Receipt" above)

Second-hand: used

Specialty store: a store that sells only a few types of items—such as lamps, jewelry, or antiques

Store credit: credit you get for returning an item

Warehouse club: a big store that sells items at lower prices

Your Mail

International

Return address

Air Mail stamp

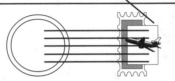

Tomiko Yamada
1716 Woodmont Ave.
Bethesda, MD 20814
U.S.A.

Air Mail

Miss Akiko Yamada
7-3-6 Kyodo, Setagaya-ku
Tokyo, Japan F156

City, Country

Domestic

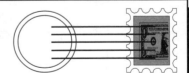

Tomiko Yamada
1716 Woodmont Ave.
Bethesda, MD 20814

Mr. Thomas Barett
066 Berkeley Ave.
Albany, CA 94706

City, State (California), Zip Code

Getting to the Post Office

Location. Most post offices have a U.S. flag near them and the words "U.S. Post Office" on the building.

Services. At the post office you can:

- mail letters and packages.
- buy stamps and supplies—such as envelopes and boxes.
- buy money orders.
- rent a post office box.

How to pay. You can pay with:

- cash.
- a check. You will need an ID— such as a driver's license.
- a credit card.

 The post office is usually open Monday through Friday from 8 or 8:30 am–5 pm and on Saturday mornings until 12 noon or 1 pm.

Domestic Mail

Ways to send

First class. This is the most common way to send letters and postcards. Mail usually arrives in 2–3 days, depending on the distance.

Fourth class ("parcel post"). Regular mail service for packages that weigh one pound (lb.) or more. Packages may take up to 8 days to arrive.

Book rate. A lower rate for sending books, records, and magazines.

Express. Overnight mail.

Priority. First-class mail that weighs over 11 ounces.

Collect-On-Delivery (COD or CASH in some countries). You pay for an item when the letter carrier delivers it to you.

 Do not mail cash; if the money gets lost, you will not be able to replace it. Use a check or money order.

Note: You may insure any package for a small fee. Ask the clerk at the post office.

How to mail a domestic letter

1. Write the addressee's name, street address, city, state, and zip code.

2. Write your own address in the upper left-hand corner of the envelope.

If you have the wrong address, the letter carrier will return the letter.

To mail a letter or package in the U.S., you must write the zip code. The zip code is a 5- or 9-digit number that shows the U.S. postal area. To find the zip code for an address, call any post office or go there and use the *Zip Code Directory*.

3. Buy a stamp if you are sending the letter regular first class.

You can buy stamps at any post office or at some supermarkets. (For certified or registered letters, go to the post office.)

4. Put your letter in a *blue* mailbox.

You can find these boxes:

- on the street—especially near the post office.
- at airports.
- in shopping malls.

Note: Read the words on the box. Some mailboxes are only for express mail.

You may also leave your letter in the mailbox outside your door or the mail slot in the door of your house; the letter carrier will pick it up.

Mailing packages

Wrap the package. Mark the box in large letters on the front and back:

- "FRAGILE" for objects that could break.
- "DO NOT BEND" for photographs or documents.
- "DO NOT X-RAY" for computer disks and film.
- "PERISHABLE" for foods that might spoil.

Go to the post office. The clerk will weigh the box and put on the postage.

 What if a package does not get there? The postal clerk can "put a trace on the package" to see if the postal system can find it.

International Mail

Letters/packages

 Airmail letters take about 7–10 days. A 2-lb. airmail package costs about $11–$12 and takes 5–7 days.

Express

International express mail takes 2–3 days; the number of delivery days is not guaranteed. (For guaranteed overnight delivery to another country, use a private service.)

 Some countries limit package weight. Ask the postal clerk about the rules of the country to which you are sending the package.

Private Services

Mailing

Private services do some jobs that the post office does not. For example, some services:

- pick up the mail at your door.
- mail overnight to countries outside the U.S.

You will pay a pick-up fee. Some services have letter-size mailing envelopes, but you must seal and label any boxes yourself.

How to pay. Most private services let you pay with a credit card. If you have an account with that company, you may charge it on the phone.

Other services

Wrapping. Often, private services have more packaging and office supplies than the post office. Also, the clerk will do the wrapping for you.

Mailboxes. Some private services rent mailboxes by the month. When you travel, the service will forward your mail to the city where you are staying.

Telegrams ("Mailgrams"). You may use a telegram to send a message quickly here or abroad. Western Union, the only company that sends telegrams, has an "800" service number to take orders and answer questions (see "Chapter Information" in the Appendix).

Faxing and copying. You may send faxes inside the U.S. or outside the U.S. at most private mail centers. Copies may be made at printing offices, office supply stores, libraries, private mail services, and at a few post offices. The price ranges from 5¢–25¢ a copy.

Words to Know

Book rate: a lower rate for sending books, records, and magazines

Certified mail: a type of first-class mail. You get a signed card proving that the person received the mail.

Collect-on-delivery (COD): a type of shipping from a store or catalog company. You pay for the item when you get it.

Express mail: overnight mail

First-class mail: the most common way to send letters and postcards

Fragile: an item that can break easily

Money order: a check you can buy at the post office or the bank. You can send the check in the mail.

Parcel post: regular mail service for packages that weigh one pound or more

Post office box: a locked box in the post office where your mail is kept until you pick it up

Priority mail: first-class mail that weighs more than 11 ounces

Registered mail: mail that is guaranteed special care and security

Surface mail: mail sent by ground or boat

Zip code: a 5-digit or 9-digit number that shows the U.S. postal delivery area in the United States

__Money Matters__

Your Bank Check

Joe Sanchez
Marie Sanchez
701 Montgomery Place
Bethesda, MD 20814

3/5 _____ 19 _93__   0001

PAY TO THE
ORDER OF _International Center_____ $ 42.76

_Forty-two dollars and 76/100_____ DOLLARS

Washington Bank
1 Pleasant Street
Washington, D.C. 20005

FOR ____tapes_____   _Joe Sanchez_

0000000   9987654321

Your Check Register

Check No.	Date	Payee	Payment	Deposit	Balance
0001	3/5	Int'l Ctr	$42.76		$ 96.12
	3/6	Transfer		$200	$296.12
0002	3/6	Giant	$31.19		$264.93

International Transactions

 Wiring money. To wire money, you may pay:

- a transaction fee, or a fee for wiring the money—about $15–$75.
- a currency conversion fee, or a fee for changing from one currency to another. If you are converting from a foreign currency into U.S. dollars, this fee may be included in the exchange rate.

Check conversions. Depositing a check from a foreign bank may cost about $20-$50 a check; the cost varies according to the transaction and the individual bank. If you are converting from a foreign currency into U.S. dollars, the exchange rate usually includes the conversion fee.

Traveler's checks (see chapters on "Before You Come" and "Traveling In & Out of the U.S.").

What to look for

To compare costs, say what the transaction is and how much money is involved. Ask:

- if the bank or company can do the transaction for you.
- how long the transaction takes.
- whether the service has pick-up and delivery.

Check the fees for the transaction (see above) and the rate of exchange. Compare costs at the same time of day—preferably early morning, when European markets are open and trading.

Wiring money to the U.S.

 You will need:

- the names and addresses of the foreign bank and of your U.S. bank's main branch.
- the routing number, or electronic address, of each bank—if possible.
- your account number.
- identification (any one of the following—driver's license, passport, student card, or credit card).

The transaction takes 2–3 days for developed countries, longer for countries that do not have many international transactions.

Wiring money from the U.S.

 Some transactions can be done immediately; but wiring money to a foreign bank may take as long as four weeks—depending on the currency and the amount of the check.

In addition to the information above (see "Wiring money to the U.S."), you will need:

- the account number of the bank you are wiring to and the name on the account.
- the date you want the currency to be exchanged.

- a cashier's check for some transactions; you probably will not need a cashier's check if you are using a bank that has your account.

Banking

Why you need a bank account

If you are going to stay for more than one or two months, you need a checking account. You may use your account to pay:

- monthly bills—for example, bills for the phone, gas and electricity, cable TV, and rent.
- grocery bills. Most supermarkets give you a courtesy card for cashing checks (see chapter on "Food Shopping").
- day-to-day expenses—such as dry cleaning and home cleaning services.

 Do not carry large amounts of cash (over $100). Pay with traveler's checks, a bank check, or a credit card.

Kinds of institutions

If you are wiring money to or from the U.S. you may use a foreign currency dealer—especially if you do not have an account with a U.S. bank.

The U.S. has three main kinds of banking institutions for other types of banking:

- banks.

- savings and loans (S&Ls).
- credit unions.

All three have the same basic services. Banks and S&Ls are private corporations, but credit unions are owned by the members themselves. Usually, you can get a loan or a credit card more easily from a credit union than from a bank.

You may join a credit union only if you are a part of a group that has one. Many large institutions have credit unions for their employees.

Choosing a bank

Services. Be sure that your branch can do the transactions you want. For example, if you will be transferring money to your home country, make sure your branch can do international transactions easily. If you will need a loan or a credit card, ask if your bank will give you one (see chapter on "Credit Cards and Loans").

Federally insured (FDIC, FSLIC, or CUIC). Most banking institutions are federally insured. If the institution fails, the U.S. government will give you up to $100,000 of your money back.

Convenience. Make sure you can do transactions easily—with an automatic teller machine (ATM) or by telephone. If you need to visit the bank often, it should be close to where you live or work.

Correspondent relationships. You will get some services more easily from a bank that has a correspondent relationship with a bank in your home country (see "What to Find Out" in chapter on "Before You Come").

Comparing banks

Many people simply use the most convenient bank; but you may want to compare:

- interest rates. All banks pay interest for savings accounts. Some pay interest for personal checking accounts, too.
- cost of services. Many banks charge fees for services such as using the ATM of another bank. Find out what fees you pay and how much they cost.
- overdraft protection. If you have overdraft protection, the bank will "honor," or pay for, a check when you overdraw your account. Without overdraft protection, your check will "bounce"; you will pay a fee—sometimes as high as $25.
- the minimum balance. The minimum balance is the least amount of money you must keep in the account. If you have less, you pay extra fees.

 To open an account, you will need money to deposit. Most banks require about $100 for each account.

Call ahead to find out what documents you need. For example, you probably will need:

- proof of your name and address. Use
  - a letter or bill sent to your home or office address.
    - a work or student ID card.
- your Social Security card or number; diplomats may need other proof that they are here as residents.
- your visa and passport.
- your employer's name and address or your student ID.
- a driver's license or other photo ID if you have one.

Most banks open from 9 am to 2–3 pm; in some areas, banks are also open at least one night a week or on Saturdays. To do everyday transactions, you may use the ATM or the drive-through window (see "Using the ATM"). The best time to open an account is Monday through Thursday mornings. It should take 30–60 minutes.

How to open an account.

1. Ask for the "new accounts" person at the bank.

You will decide:

- which accounts to use. You will probably open both a savings and a checking account.
- whether each account will be single (for one person) or joint (for more than one person).

If you have more than $100,000, ask how all your money can be federally insured.

2. **Fill out a form for each account.**

3. **Make a deposit.**

4. **Choose your checks.**

Decide what will be printed on your checks (name, address, phone number). You will get temporary checks to use until the printed ones come in the mail (about 7-10 days).

5. **Get a personal identification number (PIN).**

This is the code for using the ATM .

Using your checkbook

Check register. Record every deposit and withdrawal in the check register.

Bank statement. At the end of each month, you will get a statement listing:

- all your transactions.
- the interest earned.
- the service charges.
- a beginning and ending balance.

Check this information against your register and make any corrections.

Check clearance. When you deposit a check, you may be able to use $100 of the money right away. The rest of the money has to "clear." By law, banks must "clear," or let you use the money for:

- a local check in two days.
- an out-of-state check in five days.

- an out-of-state check for over $5,000 in nine days.

Checks from other countries may take as long as three weeks to clear.

Using the ATM

The ATM is convenient because it lets you make transactions:

- 24 hours a day, seven days a week.
- at another bank's machine with the same network.

To use an ATM, you will need a card and a PIN. You will decide your PIN when you open your account. The card comes in the mail about a week later.

 Your PIN is confidential. It is the number you need to make transactions on the ATM. Do not tell strangers this number. Do not write the number on the ATM card.

Be sure to take both your card and your receipt when you are finished. If you leave your card in an ATM, call the bank as soon as possible.

 What if I lose my card? Call the bank right away so no one else can use it. You will get a new card.

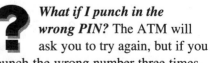 *What if I punch in the wrong PIN?* The ATM will ask you to try again, but if you punch the wrong number three times, the ATM may keep your card. Call the bank to get your card back.

Words to Know

Automatic teller machine (ATM): a machine for transactions such as depositing and withdrawing money

Balance: the amount of money in the account

Bounced check: a check you cannot cash because there is not enough money in the account

Cashier's check: a check made out by the bank

Checking account: an account in which to keep money for writing checks

Correspondent (bank): having a special relationship with a bank from another country. For example, a bank in France may have a correspondent bank in the U.S.; if you are a customer of the French bank, you may be able to get faster and better service from the correspondent bank in the U.S.

Credit card: a plastic card used to buy things; you get the bill later

Credit union: a type of banking institution. You can join only if you belong to a certain group, such as a group of employees.

Deposit: to place money in an account; the money placed in an account

Federally insured: (deposits that are) guaranteed by the federal government

Interest: money the bank pays you for keeping money in its account(s); money you pay for borrowing

Interest rate: a percentage paid for the use of money

Network (ATM): a system of connected ATMs

Overdraft protection: a way of making sure all the checks you write are cashed—even when you don't have enough money in the account

Overdraw: to write checks for more money than is in the account

Personal identification number (PIN): the number, or code, for using the ATM

Savings account: an account in which to keep money you are saving

Savings and loan (S&L): a banking institution specializing in home mortgages

Service charge: money paid to a bank for a specific job, such as cashing a check

Transaction: an exchange of money; a deposit, withdrawal, or transfer

Paying
Your Taxes

Income Tax
- U.S.
- most states and Wasington DC
- some counties and cities

Social Security (FICA) Tax
- U.S.

Real Property Tax
- most counties and cities

Personal Property Tax
- some counties and cities

Gift and Estate Tax
- U.S.

Find out about the tax laws as soon as possible—either before you arrive or right after you get here. Tax planning often saves time and money.

The information here explains the general U.S. tax rules you need to understand; but each of these rules works differently in different situations. Ask:

- a tax professional, such as a Certified Public Accountant (CPA).
- the organization that sponsors you; it may have a tax professional who can help you.
- your advisor, if you are a student.

You will need to calculate your income and many major expenses. During the year, save all your receipts and other documents that may affect your taxes (see "End-of-the-Year Taxes" below).

Kinds of Taxes

Sales tax

You probably will pay a sales tax every time you go shopping—even to the supermarket; each state and local government has different rules. The sales tax is added onto the price of taxable items such as jewelry, automobiles, certain foods, and clothing. You may not have to pay a sales tax for many items if you work for a foreign or international organization such as an embassy or the United Nations.

 You pay sales tax only when you buy things; you do not pay any more sales taxes at the end of the year.

Income tax

 Even if you pay a small amount, or none at all, you usually must "file a return"; that is, you must fill out the right forms and send them to the federal government and state taxing agencies.

You probably will pay U.S. income tax if you have income from any U.S. sources. In addition to the U.S., most states and many counties and cities have an income tax. Save any records of income—such as:

- your salary, or income earned as an employee.
- consultant fees, or income earned as a non-employee consultant.
- some scholarships and fellowships.
- capital gains.
- dividends and interest.

You may not need to pay U.S. income tax if your country has an income tax treaty with the U.S. and you meet the conditions of this agreement.

 You usually pay these taxes with each paycheck; you may pay more at the end of the tax year (see "Your Paycheck" below).

Social Security

If you are working in the U.S. for a U.S. employer, both you and your employer will pay Social Security taxes under the Federal Insurance Contribution Act (FICA). You may not need to pay if:

- the U.S. has an agreement about Social Security with your home country.
- you are a student. Ask your advisor.

 You pay these taxes with each paycheck. Be sure your employer did not take out these taxes if you need not pay them.

Property tax

 You will get a bill or form in the mail for these taxes.

Real property tax. Most city and county governments tax real property, such as land or a home. If you own a home or other property, you may pay the city or county where the property is located; this tax is only for property owners—rather than renters (see chapter on "Finding a New Home"). Each city or county has its own rules and tax rate.

Personal property tax. Some city and county governments also tax large items such as cars, boats, fur coats, jewelry, stocks, and other investments. Each city or county has its own rules and tax rate.

 You pay these taxes when you receive the bill or special form from the city or county agency (see "End-of-the-Year Taxes" below).

Gift and estate taxes

If you want to give a large gift (for example, over $10,000) or leave a will, ask about these taxes.

Your Paycheck

Overview

You will pay income and Social Security taxes with each paycheck. Your paycheck shows the amount of money:

- you have earned.
- your employer has withheld, or taken out, for taxes during the year.

At the end of the tax year, you will get a W-2 form, or Wage and Tax statement, which shows the amounts earned and withheld for the year.

 Find out if your country has any agreements with the U.S. about Social Security or income taxes. If you are exempt, make sure your employer did not withhold these taxes from your paycheck.

Income taxes

Overview: At the end of the tax year, you will calculate all the taxes you owe for that year. Then you will subtract the income taxes you have already paid during the year. If you have not paid enough, you will pay more money; if you have paid too much, ask for a refund, or some money back, from the government.

Employees. Employees will fill out a W-4 form, or Withholding Allowance Certificate, right after they start their job. This form tells the amount of taxes the company should withhold, or take out, from each paycheck.

Consultants. Consultants or self-employed workers may need to estimate the taxes they owe for each time period and send the money to the U.S. government. Your state, county, or city may have rules about estimated taxes too.

Social Security (FICA)

Both you and your employer pay for Social Security—up to a certain amount for each year. The employer will:

- withhold your part of the tax amount from your paycheck.
- add the employer's part of the tax.
- send a check to the government. The money goes toward an account in your name.

End-of-the-Year Taxes

The tax year

The tax year for most taxpayers is from January 1st to December 31st. The deadline for paying your federal taxes is midnight of the next April 15th. For example, the tax deadline for income earned in 1996 is April 15th, 1997; the date and time postmarked on the envelope must be before midnight,

April 15th. Many post offices are open until midnight on April 15th so you can file, or send, your return on time.

Planning ahead

Planning ahead is important—especially if you have a high income. For example, you may want to:

- know about how much you will pay. Your tax bill may be thousands of dollars more than the amount you have already paid.
- make sure your tax bill at the end of the year will not be too large. The most common way is to withhold more money from each paycheck.
- give money to certain charities; some charitable contributions may lower your taxes.
- find out if you can save money by making certain investments— for example, buying a home or putting money in a specific type of retirement account.

 Go to the CPA as soon as you can. Do not wait past December. In March or April, most CPAs are very busy. They may charge more or may not be able to see you.

How to file your return

1. **Find out who can help you.**

If you have a high income, a tax professional may help you save time and money (see Who Can Help" below). Visit the professional as soon as you can. If you are a student, see your advisor.

2. Get the forms you need.

(See "Documents you need" below.)

3. Calculate the total taxes you owe.

Be sure the information on your forms is true. You may pay fines or other extra fees if your forms do not show all the taxes you should pay; you may even lose the right to work or stay longer in the U.S.

4. Copy all your records.

Save all records for three years; the IRS may ask to see your documents and papers if you are still in this country. Save copies of all:

- your returns.
- personal records (see "Documents you need" below).

5. Send your tax returns and a check for any taxes you owe.

Send by midnight, April 15th to the:

- Internal Revenue Service (IRS). (See "Chapter Information" in the Appendix.)
- taxing agency for your state, county, and city.

? ***What happens if I do not pay my taxes on time?*** You may pay interest for every month you are late. In some cases, you

may also pay a penalty, or other extra fees.

? ***What happens if I do not have all my documents in time?*** You must still pay your taxes by April 15th. But if you cannot fill out all the forms by that date, you may file an extension—that is, ask for more time to file, or send out, the forms.

Documents you need

Filing forms. You can get all the filing forms you need from a tax professional or from the public library. The IRS has several forms you need to file. Find out which ones to use.

Forms showing your income. By February 1st, you should get a separate form from each source of U.S. income.

Personal records. You may need to prove the information used in your filing forms with records or receipts showing:

- personal expenses proving adjustments and deductions—such as
  - some monies put in a special retirement account.
  - some trade or business expenses.
  - contributions to some charities.
  - income you received from your employer to pay for moving expenses.
  - interest on the mortgage you paid if you own a home.
- some state and local taxes. Do not include sales taxes.
- travel in and out of the U.S. Include

- the dates you have traveled into and out of the U.S. for this year.
- the total number of days you were in the U.S. during the last two years.

How Much You Pay

Status

Legal status, or visa. The type of visa is important for calculating your taxes. For example:

- students with an F, J, or M visa may pay taxes as nonresidents.
- employees of foreign governments and certain international organizations are often taxed according to special rules.

Check with a tax professional or an attorney. If you have not left the country yet, make sure you have the best type of visa for you.

Residence status. In general, your status may be "resident alien" if you:

- have a "green card" or a "pink card."
- have been in this country for more than 183 days in one tax year.

Most resident aliens:

- pay U.S. taxes on all world-wide income earned in that year; nonresident aliens pay U.S. taxes only on U.S. income sources.

- can take advantage of more deductions and exemptions than nonresident aliens.

The rules for residence status are especially complicated; for example, your tax status may not be the same as your immigration status. Ask a tax professional.

Filing status. When you fill out the forms, you will file as:

- a married individual filing a joint return for you and your spouse.
- the head of a household—that is, you are unmarried and support children or dependents.
- single, or unmarried individual.
- married individual filing a separate return.

In general, you will pay a lower rate if you are a married individual filing a joint return or if you are the head of a household.

Taxable income

Gross income. Your gross income is the total amount of income you receive during the tax year. You lower your gross income when you subtract:

- adjustments. Some adjustments are
  - business expenses you pay yourself—for example, the cost of a business trip or moving expenses.
  - investments in some retirement funds.
- deductions. Taxpayers who have few deductions may take the standard deduction. Others itemize, or list, their deductions in

Note: *This sheet is an overview; it is not a government tax form.*

Overview of Federal Income Tax

Gross income	**Start with your total income for the year.**	$ _____
(-) Adjustments	Minus adjustments	$ _____
Adjusted gross income (AGI)	**Your new total is the adjusted income.**	$ _____
(-) Deductions	Minus deductions	$ _____
(-) Exemptions	Minus exemptions	$ _____
Taxable income	**Your new total is the amount of income that can be taxed.**	$ _____
(x) Taxable income x rate	Multiply the taxable income x the rate.	$ _____
(-) Tax credits	Minus tax credits (payments such as child care or certain foreign taxes)	$ _____
Total federal income tax liability	**Your new total is the total amount of taxes you owe for the year.**	$ _____
(-) Taxes paid for the year	Minus taxes you have paid—such as those withheld from your paycheck	$ _____
Federal income taxes owed or a refund for taxes already paid	**Your new total is the amount you will pay or receive.**	$ _____

order to lower their taxes even more. Some deductions are:
  - income taxes paid to a state, county, or city in the U.S.
  - interest on home mortgages.
  - some contributions to charity.
- exemptions. Exemptions are a tax deduction ($2,500 in 1995) for
  - yourself.
  - each of your dependents.

Credits. Credits are expenses that lower your taxes—such as day care. Credits lower your taxes even more than adjustments, deductions, and exemptions; each credit dollar lowers your taxes by one dollar.

Tax bracket. In general, the greater the amount of taxable income, the higher the rate.

Getting Help

Tax professionals

A tax professional will:

- help you plan for your taxes (see "Planning ahead" above).
- calculate the total amount of taxes you owe and the amount for each tax return.
- fill out the U.S., state, and local tax forms.
- tell you when and where to send any payments.

- tell you what other papers and documents you need to save during the year.

Look for a professional who is:

- experienced in international taxes.
- a CPA or licensed attorney.
- a member of a professional association, such as the American Institute of Certified Public Accountants.

 Accountants usually charge $85–$150 an hour. Often, the first visit is free. Attorneys often charge more—sometimes up to $200 an hour.

Words to Know

Accountant (see "Certified public accountant" below)

Adjustments: a type of investment or expense that lowers your taxable income

Assets: everything you own that is worth money—such as a home, stocks and other investments, a car, or jewelry

Capital gains tax: the tax on the money you earn when you sell stocks, bonds, real property, or other investments

Certified public accountant (CPA): a licensed professional who helps you with your tax forms

---

If you plan to be in the U.S. a long time and have a high income, tax professionals can help you with a long-term plan for investments.

Deductions: expenses that reduce taxable income

Dependent: a person whom you support by using your income to pay for major living expenses—such as housing, food, and clothing. Usually, your dependent is a child, spouse, or parent who lives with you.

Disabled: unable to work for a long time because of an injury or sickness

Estate tax: the tax paid when someone dies. The tax is on all the dead person's assets—such as property and money.

Estimate: calculate the approximate amount ahead of time. Estimates are not exact; for example, when you estimate income, you calculate how much you will earn within a certain time—as best you can.

Exempt: free from. If you are tax exempt, you do not have to pay U.S. taxes.

Exemptions: a tax deduction you can take for yourself and each of your dependents. In general, the number of exemptions depends on the number of your dependents—for example, a spouse or child who needs your income for major living expenses.

Federal Government: U.S. government—rather than the state or local governments

FICA: (see "Social Security tax" below)

Gift tax: the tax someone pays when he or she gives a gift that is worth more than a certain amount of money

Gross income: the total amount of money received during the year—including your salary, scholarships, interest, and the profit from selling stocks, real property, other investments

Income tax: the tax you pay on the money you have earned during the year

Joint return: a filing status. With a joint return, you and your spouse calculate both your incomes together; the filing status helps to decide the rate you pay.

Personal property tax: the tax on items such as jewelry, fur, cars, stocks, or other investments. This tax goes to some city and state governments.

Real property tax: the tax you pay on real property—such as land, houses, or other buildings you own. This tax goes to some city and state governments.

Refund: money you get back. You get a tax refund if you have paid more than enough taxes during the year.

Residence status: your status for U.S. tax purposes—such as a "resident alien" or "nonresident alien." This status is for paying taxes only; you may have a different status for other purposes.

Sales tax: taxes you pay when you buy something

Schedule: a filing form that lists information such as all sources and amounts of income

Single return: a filing status. With a single return, you file as an unmarried person; if you are married, you and your spouse file separate forms.

Standard deduction: a fixed amount you may lower your taxable income by. You may use this deduction instead of listing expenses separately.

Social Security tax or Federal Insurance Contribution Act (FICA): the taxes you and your employer pay for a type of government insurance. The U.S. Social Security System provides benefits for retirement, old age, or disability.

Taxable income: the total amount of your income used to calculate your taxes; your gross income minus deductions and exemptions

Tax return: a form used to calculate your taxes. You must complete this form and send it to the IRS and state tax agencies.

W-2 form: The form you get from your employer at the end of the tax year. This form shows how much money you have earned and how much money has been taken out for taxes.

W-4 form: The form you fill out when you start your job. Your employer uses this form to calculate how much tax money to withhold, or take out, from each paycheck.

For More Ways to Feel At Home . . .

Visit us on the Internet, where you will find:

❑ Personal contacts and advice about the area you will live in...especially for relocating individuals and families. Helps you choose the right home in the right neighborhood, schools for your child...

❑ Personal research and advice about college applications and programs...including financial aid. Helps you get admitted to the college that is best for you.

❑ Publications list—including books about living in U.S. cities, college admissions, American customs and communications.

Find out more!
Visit us on the Internet: http://www.hellousa.com/world

Settling In

Finding a
New Home

Townhouse (rowhouse)

Apartment (condominium)

Detached house (colonial)

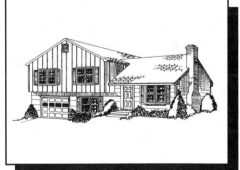

Detached house (split-level)

Residential Areas

Areas

You may live in:

- an urban area, inside a big city. First, be sure the area is safe—both day and night. Urban homes are often older with small yards; parking may be a problem. Often, urban homes are close to the bus stop or the subway station, so you may not need a car.
- a suburban area, in cities or towns near a big city. About 50% of the residents in a large metropolitan area live in the suburbs. The homes are often newer than city homes, with big yards and lots of trees. You may need a car for shopping and trips to the dry-cleaners or the post office. Check the time it takes to get to work.
- a rural area, away from cities or towns. Usually, rural homes have lots of trees and land. You probably will drive for everyday trips. Check the time it takes to get to work.

 In general, prices are highest in the areas closest to a big city. Taxes and insurance costs are higher in a city, too (see "Renting" and "Buying" below).

Types of homes

You may rent or buy a:

- detached home. The home is not attached to other homes.

- townhouse, or rowhouse. The home is attached to other homes. With a townhouse, you may pay a monthly fee for taking care of common grounds such as a grassy area in the middle or a swimming pool.
- condo. You own the apartment. Together, all the owners in the building own the common areas—such as the lobby, hallways, pools, and parking lot; owners pay monthly condo fees to take care of these areas.
- co-op. You pay the mortgage; but, by law, each owner has a share in a corporation for the building. The corporation owns all the apartments, as well as the common areas. The monthly fees are higher, but they include real estate taxes.

In general, if you rent, you do not pay any condo fees for taking care of common areas; but you can use any facilities such as a party room or pool; you may pay extra for parking.

What to look for

Safety: Walk around yourself and ask people who live in the area; be sure to go at night and during the day. Call the police crime division for the county or city to find out about crimes in that area. Look in the front of your local phone book for the number.

Schools. The different counties or cities manage the public schools. Find out which schools are best before you decide where to live (see chapters on

"Your Young Child" and "Your Older Child").

Residents/neighbors. Do you see children around? Do both husbands and wives work? If so, will you or your spouse be lonely during the day?

Transportation. If you plan to use public transportation, ask: How far is the bus or subway stop? How often do the buses run? Do they run on weekends (see chapter on "Getting Around")?

If you plan to drive, ask: How far is the main road? How heavy is the traffic when I will be driving? How long will I need to go to work or school?

Stores and other services. Does the area have good restaurants, shops, beauty salons, libraries, or houses of worship?

The Fair Housing Law

By law, no homeowner or landlord can refuse to rent or sell because of your:

- race.
- sex.
- country of origin, or the country you come from.
- religion.

In most cities, homeowners cannot refuse to rent or sell to families with children, but they can refuse to rent to families who:

- have pets.
- do not have enough money.
- have too many people for the size of the home.

If you think someone is disobeying this law, call the Office of Fair Housing and Equal Opportunity; find the number under:

- "Fair Housing" or "Housing" in the city or county government section of your phone book.
- "Housing and Urban Development" in the U.S. Government section of your phone book.

Who Can Help

The housing office of your college or employer may give you some help. Many newcomers use a real estate agent, relocation center, or rental service (see "How to rent a home" below). Most homes for rent or sale are in multiple listings; that is, they are all on one list that most real estate agents or services use.

What to look for. Pick an agent who:

- is trained. Be sure the professional is a member of an association of realtors (see "Chapter Information" in the Appendix). To be a member, the professional must be certified.
- pays attention to what you want and what you can afford.
- knows the area. If you don't know where you want to live, you may need to use several agents or go to a relocation center.
- has patience. Do not let an agent "talk you" into making a decision before you are ready.
- is experienced. How long has the agent been selling/renting homes?

Does he or she work full-time or part-time?

⊗ Many international visitors want agents who speak their own language. But also ask yourself: Would I trust this person in my own country? Is this agent experienced? Does this agent want to help me?

Renting

Rental prices vary according to the area and the type of housing. Furnished apartments and homes cost about 20%–50% more, but you may rent furniture separately at less cost. Usually, you pay a fee for the rental application. This covers the cost of the credit check.

Many single men or women rent:

- a basement apartment in a rowhouse.
- a room in a family home. Usually, you get
  - a private bedroom and bathroom.
  - the use of a washer and dryer.
  - the use of the kitchen to prepare your meals.
- a house or an apartment with a roommate. Some cities have services that help you find a roommate; all types of people use these services—including students, young professionals, and executives. You will pay a fee for the service—often, under $50. Look in the Yellow Pages under "Roommate."

How much you can afford

In general, do not spend more than 28%–33% of your income on monthly payments—including the rental fee, parking and association fees, and insurance. If you owe a lot of money, your monthly payments should be less.

📁 When you apply for a lease, you will show your driver's license or other photo ID. If you are a student, you may not need any more letters or documents. Others may also need information such as:

- the name of your employer or school.
- proof of income—for example, some proof of the amount you expect to earn this year; you may not need this if you are a student.
- the address where you lived before .
- the name of your landlord (if you lived in the U.S.).
- local references, if possible (your employer, embassy, or sponsor).
- the name of your local bank.

Some apartments in many large cities are rent-stabilized or rent-controlled; that is, the landlord cannot raise the rent more than a certain amount every year. In general, these apartments are less expensive for the space. The laws are different in every city. For example, in New York City, only apartments built before 1974 may be rent-stabilized or rent-controlled.

How to rent a home

1. Begin your search.

You may get information from:

- real estate agents. Many real estate agents both sell and rent homes. Most prefer to sell rather than rent, but some housing professionals specialize in rentals.
- newspaper advertisements.
- housing magazines. Often, you can find these free magazines near a bank machine (ATM) or in special boxes on the street.
- apartment search companies. These companies have offices in many metropolitan areas. The workers there can tell you about the kinds of apartments around. The services are free.

2. Meet with the housing professional helping you.

During the meeting, the agent or broker will:

- ask what kind of home and community you want.
- ask about your salary and the money in your bank account. Then the agent will tell you how much you are "qualified," or able to pay.
- give you listings of homes you might like.

3. Visit the places you have chosen.

Most agents will drive you to the homes; rental services give directions. The owner will probably not be there; but you can ask the agent or rental office questions.

4. Try to negotiate the price.

Apartments owned by a business often have a fixed price; but private owners may be willing to negotiate. Sometimes, you may be able to negotiate a month of free parking or a lower rental rate.

5. Read the lease; if you don't understand it, have someone else translate it.

Be sure everything you expect to get is in the lease; for example, if the agent told you the rent includes parking, the lease should say so.

6. Fill out the application form and pay the application fee.

7. Sign the lease.

8. Make your first payment.

This payment includes the security (or damage) deposit—usually equal to one month's rent. After you move out, the owner or manager will inspect the home. If everything is in good order, you will get your deposit back. If you have caused some damage, your deposit will pay for repairs.

Find out if you can "break the lease," or leave early, if you want to. If you need to break the lease, you may have to pay—usually 1 or 2 months' rent, but maybe more. You may also have to give notice, or tell the landlord that you are leaving ahead of time. The number of weeks' or months' notice should be in the lease.

The lease

The lease should include:

- the amount of the deposit.
- the amount of the rent.
- the day you must pay the rent.
- a list of any other payments you must make.
- a list of any extras, such as the use of a washer and dryer.
- the rules for breaking a lease or moving out early (see the warning above).
- any other rules you must fol-low—such as not having pets.
- any fees or costs the landlord pays—such as utilities, lawn services, pest control, or repairs.

Monthly payments

Rent. This is the largest payment.

Insurance. Insurance protects you in case of fire or theft (see chapter on "Insurance").

Utilities. Rental payments sometimes include utility costs. Check with the real estate agent for average costs.

Parking fees. If you live in an apart-ment or condominium (condo), you may have parking fees.

Water and sewage. Check with your real estate agent.

Telephone. You will pay a monthly fee for the basic telephone service. This fee is less than $20; extra features and long-distance calls add to the cost. (see chapters on "Moving In" and "The Telephone").

 What if the landlord does not follow the terms of the lease— for example, if he does not fix a broken pipe? If necessary, call the local office of Landlord-Tenant Rela-tions for your county or city. Look in the county or city government section of your phone book under "Housing." If the number is not listed, call the general number and ask.

Buying

When to buy

In most areas, you will lose money if you buy a home and then sell it in 1-2 years. Check:

- the price of homes. Are they rising, falling, or staying the same?
- the cost of selling. You will pay fees to the real estate agent and for closing costs (see below).

If you do not know when you will be moving again, rent first.

How much you can afford

In general, do not spend more than 28%–33% of your salary on the monthly payments—mortgage principal, interest, property taxes, and insurance. As with rentals, this percentage can change according to your debts or taxes.

 When buying a home, remember the closing costs and other fees you pay right away. These fees include the cost of a lawyer, points (special loan fees), homeowner's insurance, and the loan application fee. For example, closing costs for a $200,000 home may be $2,000 or more. Often, the bank or the seller will agree to pay some of these costs. Negotiate.

Types of agents

The two types of real estate agents are (see "Chapter Information" in the Appendix"):

- a seller's agent. Most agents are seller's agents—that is, they work for the seller, not the buyer. In many areas, they must tell the seller your "highest price," or the most you will pay—information you probably don't want the seller to know.
- a buyer's agent. Some agents work only for the buyer, not the seller. A buyer's agent usually gets a fee from the buyer. You will get this money back when you buy a home.

Ask if the agent will help you:

- negotiate the best deal.
- find out everything—both good and bad—about the home and the area.

Monthly expenses

Principal and interest. This mortgage payment is the largest expense of owning a home.

Taxes. The amount depends on where you live and the cost of the home. For example, in 1995, school and property taxes for $250,000 home in one suburb near San Francisco were about $3,600 a year; the same taxes for a $250,000 home in one suburb of Atlanta, GA were about $2,500 a year.

Insurance. The cost of your insurance depends on:

- the cost of your home.
- the age of your home.
- the location of your home; insurance for homes in a big city usually cost more.
- the construction and materials in your home.
- the use of safety devices—such as a burglar alarm system.

Condominium or homeowner's association fees. If you buy a townhouse or condominium, you will pay a monthly maintenance fee. The fee for some condos may be $400 a month for keeping the building clean. For other condos, the fee may be $1,000–$2,000 a month; this fee usually includes a 24-hour door person, swimming pool, health club, and tennis courts.

See "Renting" above for costs of utilities, parking, and telephone payments.

Words to Know

Application fee: money you pay for someone to look at your application

Buyer's agent: a real estate professional who helps a buyer find a home. This agent works for the buyer, not the seller.

Closing costs: fees you pay when you sign the mortgage

Condominium (condo): one of many homes in a building. Usually, each condo is owned by the person who lives in it or who rents it to someone else. All the owners together own the common areas—such as the hallways, pool, or party room.

Condominium association fees: money you pay for the care of the condo building

Co-op: one of many homes in a building. Each landlord or resident pays a separate mortgage; but all the owners together are part of a corporation that

---

Abbreviations

You will see these abbreviations in the classified ads for places to rent or buy.

Appt:	Appointment	**Ht:**	Heat
Apt:	Apartment	**Immed:**	Immediate
Balc:	Balcony	**Incl:**	Included
Bdrm (or BR):	Bedroom	**Kit:**	Kitchen
Bsmt:	Basement	**Lbr:**	Library
CAC:	Central air conditioning	**Prkg avail:**	Parking available
CATV:	Cable television	**Redec:**	Redecorated
DR:	Dining room	**Refs req:**	References requested
D/W:	Dishwasher	**TH:**	Townhouse
Effcy:	Efficiency	**Utils:**	Utilities
Elec:	Electricity	**W/D:**	Washer and dryer
Hdwd flrs:	Hardwood floors	**W/W:**	Wall-to-wall carpeting

owns each of the homes and the common areas.

Detached house: a home that is not attached to another house

Efficiency: a small apartment—usually with one main room, a kitchen, and a bathroom (see "Studio" below)

Homeowner's association fees: money you pay for front desk service, swimming pool, etc.

Insurance: a way to protect your belongings and property

Lease: a written agreement between a tenant and landlord

Mortgage: the monthly payment a homeowner makes to the bank. This payment usually includes the principal and interest of the loan.

Points: the fee you pay for a loan

Principal: money a bank lends you

Qualified: able to afford, or to pay

Real estate agent (realtor): a housing professional who can help you find a home to buy or rent

References: your employer or another person who can give the bank information about your job, income, or ability to pay

Relocation center: a place with professionals that help you find a home and learn about the area

Rentals: rooms, apartments, or houses you rent rather than buy

Rent-controlled or rent-stabilized: an apartment with rent that is regulated by the city; the landlord can raise the rent only a certain percentage every year

Rowhouses: houses that are attached to each other on the sides, usually found in the city

Rural: an area in the country (not near a city)

Security deposit: money paid to a landlord before a place can be rented. You get this money back if you do not damage the house in any way.

Seller's agent: a real estate professional who helps someone sell a house. This agent works for the seller, not the buyer.

Studio: a one-room residence with a kitchen and bath

Suburb: an area where people live near a city. For instance, Marietta outside of Atlanta and Lake Forest outside of Chicago.

Townhouses: homes that are attached to each other at the sides, usually found in the suburbs

Utilities: services such as electricity, gas, water, sewage, and heating oil

_____Moving In_____

4 weeks before you move	**Buy insurance.**	**Visit your new home.** **Check the fire alarms.** **Decide how to decorate.**
2 weeks before you move	**Tell the post office you are moving.**	**Call your local phone company for new service.** **Call a long-distance company for long-distance service.**
1 week before you move	**Call to arrange for:** **electricity/ gas.** **water/ sewage.** **cable TV.** **heating oil (if necessary).** **the elevator. Reserve (if necessary).**	
1-2 days before you move	**Call the moving company to confirm all arrangements.**	

Before You Move

Insurance

Everyone who rents or owns a home needs home insurance. Buy it as soon as you can (see chapter on "Insurance").

Post office

At the post office, get:

- a "Change of Address" card. This card tells the post office to send any mail to your new home for one year.
- some "Change of Address" cards. Send a card with your new address to any person, publication, or office that sends you mail.

Telephone service

You will need a local telephone company for calls in your metropolitan area and a long-distance company for all other calls. For example, you will need a long-distance company to call from New York City to San Francisco. Find out about long-distance companies before you move in (see chapter on "Telephone Services and Equipment").

Utilities

 Be sure the heater and the air conditioner are safe. In some cities, homes often have heaters in the attic; these heaters may be unsafe. Ask a professional to inspect the heater for safety. If you are renting, your landlord usually hires someone. If you are buying, you will hire an inspector to look over the whole house—including the heater and air conditioner (see chapter on "Finding a New Home").

"Utilities" are services such as electricity, gas, water and sewage, and heating oil. In some condos or townhouses, the condo fees pay for these services. In most homes, you must pay.

 Most companies need to know 3-7 days ahead of time. Look for the telephone number of the public utility in the city or county government section of your phone book. Find the number for the local utilities company under "Public Utilities," "Electric Services," "Gas," or "Utilities" in the Yellow Pages.

 How do I pay for utilities? You get a bill each month. Some services may be free.

 You may need to pay a deposit for each utility. This deposit is returned at the end of the year or when you move again.

Electricity. Ask the utility company about its energy-saving programs. If you use one of these programs, you get a discount on your monthly bill.

Heating oil and gas. If you have an oil-burning furnace, contact a local oil supply company. Find the number in the Yellow Pages under "Gas Companies."

 Before you move in, check with the person who lived there before about the cost.

Many gas companies offer plans to save heat and lower costs; if you like, your gas company will visit your home to explain these plans.

Water and sewage. Find the number under "Water and Sewage Service" in the Yellow Pages. Make sure your water is turned on and your house is connected to a sewer.

Furniture

Find furniture stores in the Yellow Pages under:

- "Furniture-New."
- "Furniture-Rental."
- "Furniture-Used."

For used furniture, also check:

- the classified advertisements in the newspaper under listings such as "Merchandise Mart," "Apartment & Moving Sales," "Garage Sales," and "Estate Sales."
- flea markets. Some have the same hours each week. Others come for 1-2 days every once in a while.
- yard sale signs in your neighborhood. Friday, Saturday, and Sunday are the best days. You may try to bargain at these sales.

TV cable service

You may get cable TV in most areas. The cable gives you:

- more channels to watch (see chapter on "News, Sports, and Entertainment").

- better video and sound if your channels are not coming in clearly.

If you live in an apartment building, first ask the building manager if the building is wired for cable TV. To have cable TV installed in your home, call the cable company for your area. Ask the company for:

- booklets that explain the kind of programs on each cable channel.
- a sample cable guide.
- the cost (see below).

 Make sure you get a price list for each service; also ask about discounts or "specials."

Your Pet

You probably have to license your dog; you may also have to license a cat or other animal. Dogs and outdoor cats in most cities must wear tags with the date of their last rabies vaccination; otherwise, Animal Control will pick them up.

Ask your local Department of Animal Control about:

- licensing.
- neutering laws. In some cities or counties, you may get a discount if your pet is "fixed" so it cannot reproduce.
- leash laws.
- vaccinations against certain diseases.

Fines, or penalty fees, for unlicensed pets may be as high as $100.

Moving Inside the U.S.

 Keep everything safe from thieves—especially if you are moving yourself. Keep the moving truck locked at all times, especially when you walk away from it. If the move takes more than one day:

- do not keep your furniture and other things in the truck overnight.
- buy a time-activated light for the empty house.

The cheapest way to move is to rent a van or a truck and move yourself.

To hire a moving company, call three weeks or more before you move (see "International Movers" in chapter on "Before You Come"; this section will help you prepare for a move and choose a moving company). If you need to move soon, try to move:

- between the 7th and 10th days of the month; you may be able to get a mover in 1–3 days.
- in the middle of the month; you may be able to get a mover in about 1 week.

Start early in the morning; some movers charge more after 5 pm. The cost usually depends on the:

- number of hours worked.
- number of people working.
- weight of the furniture and boxes.
- distance between the two homes.
- driving time from one home to another.

Tip the movers $5–$10 for each worker for a move that takes 1–2 days.

After You Move

Trash collection

Trash pick-up may be free; most places charge homeowners a monthly or annual fee. Ask about these costs and services before you move.

If the local government does not pick up the garbage on your street, you must buy the service from the company in your area.

Street pick-up. Put your trash in plastic bags, tightly tied at the top. Put the bags in a plastic or metal can with a lid on top. Leave the cans or bags near the street curb the night before or early in the morning (by 7 am) on pick-up day. Make sure that raccoons or other animals cannot get into the trash; if the trash is spilled on the street, the garbage service will not pick it up.

Large items. The regular service probably does not pick up large items—such as sofas, refrigerators, or mattresses. Most communities have two or three "major clean-up" days when you can throw away large items.

To throw out the items right away, call the number of your trash service. Find the number in the city or county government section of your phone book under "Trash Collection Services." If it isn't listed, call "General Information" for your city or county.

Recycling. In most communities, you put newspapers, glass and plastic bottles, aluminum cans, and other items in a separate box for recycling. Other communities have centers where you take these items. To call, find the number in the county or city government section of your phone book under "Recycling" or "General Information."

Apartment buildings and condominiums. Most have a trash room on each floor. Ask the building manager about recycling.

Fire alarm systems

In most communities, every home must have a smoke detector on each floor or level of the building. The detector makes a loud noise if smoke is in the air. If your smoke detector runs on batteries, it will make a noise when it needs new batteries. Some people replace these batteries every year—just to be safe.

You should also have a fire extinguisher in each level of your home—especially the kitchen. You can buy them at a hardware store.

Home Services

Home decorating

You may hire a private decorator or you may use a personal decorator from a store (see chapter on "Shops & Malls").

Lawn care

If your new home has a lawn, ask if your landlord hires someone to take care of it. If not, you are responsible. You may hire a lawn-care company to do all the yard work. Some companies give discounts if many people on the same street use them.

Housekeeping

You may get a housecleaning company or an individual housekeeper. With a company, one or more people come at the same time. Most cleaning companies are bonded; that is, they will pay if anything is damaged or stolen.

Individual housekeepers often cost less than the companies and will do more types of jobs than other services. With individual housekeepers, you may need to pay Social Security taxes; ask an accountant.

Extermination

In some areas, you need an exterminator to keep out mice or bugs. For example, residents in Miami need an exterminator to keep out termites—bugs that eat wood and may harm your home. If you are renting, the landlord may hire an exterminator to come in once a month.

Snow Plowing

If your area gets snow in the winter, you may hire someone for the season. The contractor will plow your sidewalk, driveway, and the paths around the house. In some places, you may also hire a young person to do the shoveling or plowing for you.

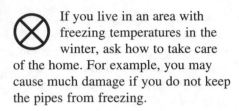 If you live in an area with freezing temperatures in the winter, ask how to take care of the home. For example, you may cause much damage if you do not keep the pipes from freezing.

Alarm Security System

Alarm security systems let you know if a robber is trying to get into your house. If your home already has a system, you pay every month to keep the service. Installing a new system may cost $1000 or more; ask your neighbors if you need one.

Words to Know

Alarm security system: a system in your house that warns you if someone is trying to get in

Appraisal: a professional estimate that tells how much something is worth. You ask a professional appraiser to tell you how much items such as jewelry or furniture are worth so you can take out the right amount of insurance.

Deposit: money you pay before a service starts

Extermination service: a service that gets rid of mice, rats, and bugs

Flea market: an open area where people sell items on tables or in tents.

Flea markets are good for items such as antiques, furniture, jewelry, audio and video cassettes, and clothing such as jackets and hats.

Hardware store: a store that sells many items for the home—such as tools, light bulbs, door knobs, and wooden shelves

Leash laws: laws about keeping your pet on a leash, attached to you, or tied up

License tag: a small metal tag to put on your pet's collar to show it is registered with the city

Neutering: "fixing" your pet so that it doesn't reproduce

Recycling: to make new products from old cans, bottles, plastic, and paper

Sewage: the pipes that take water out of your house

Smoke detector: an alarm in your home. It makes a loud sound if smoke is in the air.

Snow plowing: clearing the road, driveway, or path of snow. The city or town plows the streets; you shovel or plow your sidewalk, driveway, and the paths around the house.

Utilities: services such as electricity, gas, water, sewage, and heating oil

Telephone Services & Equipment

Leaving a message

Answering machine: "You have reached the office of Henry Marvin. I'm either on the phone or away from my desk. Please leave your name, number, and a brief message. I'll get back to you as soon as possible."

Sophia (hears a long beep sound on the phone): Hello, this is Sophia Césare. I'm calling to confirm my interview with you for tomorrow, June 25th at 2 pm. If you have a problem with this date or time, please call me back to reschedule. I'll be in my office all day until 5 pm. My number is 710-9999.

Note: Sophia gives the reason she is calling. She leaves her number and gives a good time to call back.

Ordering Phone Service

Local service

Most cities have only one local phone company. When you get phone service in your home, you will decide:

- how to be listed in the phone book; that is
  - how you spell your name.
  - if the names of both the husband and wife will be listed.
- if you want a flat rate or per-call service (see "Regular service plans" below).
- which features you want (see "Special services" below).

You may decide not to be listed at all; that is, your number will not be in the phone book and directory assistance will not tell anyone your number.

Regular service plans. Ask about the different plans. The most popular are:

- unlimited (flat rate) service. All local calls are free. Most people use this service.
- per-call (measured or message rate) service. The monthly price is less than the flat rate service, but your total bill may be more if you make a lot of calls. Usually, this plan is good for a person who makes only 2-3 calls per day.

Special services. Most large community phone companies offer many special features. You may have a connection fee for each service. The monthly fee for each service is about $3–$7. Some services offered are:

- Answer Call. Takes messages when you do not answer the phone. "Answer Call" has some advantages over buying an answering machine (see "Telephone Equipment" below).
- Call Waiting. Lets you get a second call while you are already on the phone. You may put the first caller on "hold;" that is, the first caller waits while you answer another call. You may also get a phone that has a special button for "Call Waiting."
- Call Forwarding. Lets you get calls at another number. For example, you may forward your calls to an answering service or to your office.
- 3-way Calling. Lets you talk to three people on three separate lines at the same time.
- Multiple lines. Lets you have different telephone numbers on one phone.
- Redial. Lets you redial the last number you called, or tried to call, by pressing one button.
- Speed dialing. Lets you store several numbers in the phone. When you call one of these numbers, you press only one button. If you get a phone that has "speed dialing," you will not need this service from your telephone company.
- Voice Mail (see "Answer Call" above). In some areas, Voice Mail may give businesses more services for sending and receiving messages inside the building.

Telephone books

When you move into your new home, you usually get two telephone books— the White Pages and the Yellow Pages; sometimes, you may get one book with both kinds of pages. The front part of the White Pages has information about:

- the different rates and services— for example, the prices of the different plans and special services (see "Local service" above).
- using the telephone—for example, different ways to pay your bill and numbers to call if your phone service isn't working well.

Long-distance service

To make a call outside of the local calling area, order service from a long-distance phone company. All the large long-distance companies have long-distance service for calls inside and outside the U.S.; if you want to use a smaller company, make sure you can make international calls.

Call two or three different companies and ask about their plans (see "Chapter Information" in the Appendix). Compare services and prices. Find out the rates for the places you call most often. Also ask about the company's plans for international calls.

"Translation" calls

Your long-distance telephone company may be able to translate any phone call for you as an extra service (see "Translation Services" in chapter on "When You Arrive").

Telephone Equipment

Phones

Overview. You may rent telephones from AT&T (see chapter on "Moving In"). You may buy phones from telephone or electronic stores. If you are staying in the U.S. for more than a few months, you probably will save money if you buy a phone.

There are two kinds of phones: touch tone and dial (rotary); in general, rotary phones are older than touch tone phones.

 You will pay $10–$40 or more for a phone, depending on how many "extras" you want.

Touch tone (push button). Most phones are touch tone; with this phone, you make a call by pressing the number buttons. With a rotary (pulse) phone, you dial instead. Rotary phones are usually older.

To find the telephone numbers of businesses and residents in other cities, buy a CD-ROM with the phonebook listings of all major U.S. cities.

Touch tone phones have many advantages—such as:

- Pressing the buttons is faster.
- You may do some kinds of business only with a touch tone phone—for example, banking by telephone.
- You must have a touch tone phone to use certain phone services, such as Answer Call.

Speaker phone. Many phones let you hear and talk to someone on the phone through a speaker; you may keep the receiver on the phone, so that several people can listen to a call at one time. Speaker phones also let you write or read more easily while you are on the phone.

Cordless (portable) phone. The receiver has no wires; so you do not have to stay in one place while you are on the phone.

Phone/fax machine. The phone also serves as a facsimile (fax) machine.

Cellular (wireless) phone. These are especially popular for use in the car. You will pay for:

- cellular phone service for a set period of time (6 months-1 year). The cost is about $30 a month.
- an activation charge.
- each call you make or receive.

Other features. You may choose a phone with:

- **conference calls.** Conferencing lets you talk to more than two people at one time.
- **an "on hold" button** (see "Local service" above).

- **a long cord.** You may want a long cord so you can walk around the room while you are talking.
- **the color and style you want.** You may choose any color you want. One popular style is the "princess phone."

Answering machines

Most Americans have answering machines or use the Answer Call feature (see "Special services" above). You may buy an answering machine at a department or discount store or a phone or electronic store. The cheapest machines cost about $25.

 Which is better—an answering machine or the Answer Call Service? An answering machine may cost less; but answer call has many advantages—such as:

- You may forward your calls, or send them to the phone where you will be.
- Callers may leave messages when the line is busy. That way, you do not miss an important call just because you are on the phone.

Words to Know

Answer Call (or "Call Answering"): an "extra" service that lets you get messages when you do not answer

Call Forwarding: an "extra" service that lets you send your calls to another number

Call Waiting: an "extra" service that lets you switch to another caller while you are on the phone with someone

Cellular phone: a wireless phone—such as a car phone

Connection fee: the money you pay to start your phone service

Cordless phone: a kind of phone. The receiver is not attached to the main part of the phone.

Flat rate: a kind of basic service. The price for this service is the same every month; you can make as many local calls as you want at no extra cost.

Hold: to wait. To put someone "on hold" is to have that person wait on the phone while you talk to someone else.

Measured rate: a basic phone service. Each month, you can make a certain number of local calls for "free." Then you pay extra for each call.

Per-call service: (see "Measured rate" above)

Pulse phone: a kind of phone. You dial the numbers to make a call.

Push button phone: a kind of telephone. You press the buttons with numbers on them.

Rotary phone: (see "Pulse phone" above)

Speaker phone: a phone with which you can hear and talk to someone without holding the receiver

Speed dialing: an "extra" service. It lets you call certain numbers fast.

Touch tone phone: (see "Push button phone" above)

Unlimited rate: (see "Flat rate" above)

Voice Mail: an "extra" service that lets you get messages when you do not answer the phone. Voice Mail is like Answer Call (see above); but it may have more services for sending and receiving messages for businesses.

White Pages: the telephone book that lists people's names and home numbers

Yellow Pages: the telephone book that has advertisements for products and services

Insurance You Need

 Medical

Medical: visits to the doctor, lab tests, hospital stays, surgery, ambulance, treatment (medicine, therapy)*

Dental: visits to the dentist, X-rays, and treatments such as fillings, cleanings, oral surgery

Medical evacuation:* transportation to your home country if you get sick and cannot continue your studies or work here

Repatriation of mortal remains:* transportation of your body to your home country if you die

Home and Property

Personal property: the value of personal property such as furniture, electronic equipment, and jewelry if damaged, lost, or stolen

Liability: medical costs of an injury to a visitor on your property or in your home

Homeowners' (only for people who own their own home): repairs to your home if it is damaged or the value of your home if it is destroyed

 Auto

Collision: repairs to your car if it is damaged or the value of your car if it is destroyed

Liability:* injuries to people hurt in an accident when you are the driver of the car

Comprehensive: repairs to your car or the value of your car if it is damaged or destroyed when no one is driving it.

* required by the U.S. government for several types of visas
** required by most states in order to drive a car

Note: This page lists only the major types of insurance; ask your agent if you need other types of policies. Also note that you may not need all the types here. For example, you may not need collision for an old car; again, ask your agent.

Overview

Why you need it

While you are in the U.S., you need insurance in case:

- you become sick or injured.
- you cause someone else to become sick or injured.
- your home or any other property is damaged or stolen.
- you cause someone else's property to be damaged.

If you are just visiting here for a short time, your medical insurance from home may still protect you. If not, you probably can get special travel insurance; but you will need more insurance if you:

- live or stay here more than a few months.
- buy, rent, or lease a car.
- buy or rent a house or apartment.

 In many countries, the government pays for the medical care of its citizens. In the U.S., most individuals and families are responsible for their own medical care. This care is expensive; for example, one night in a hospital usually costs $1000 or more.

Without insurance, you may not be able to pay your medical bills if you get sick or injured. Some hospitals or doctors may not treat you if you do not have insurance. If you will be in the U.S. for more than a few months, be sure you can get medical insurance while you are still in your home country. If you are here already, get medi-cal insurance for yourself and your family right away.

How the system works

When you buy insurance, you pay a premium regularly—for example:

- monthly (every month).
- quarterly (every three months).
- semi-annually (twice a year).
- annually (every year).

In return, you get paid back for certain costs —for example, medical costs.

The insurance company puts all the premiums together into a "pool." When you have an expense for which you are insured, you make a claim to the company; that is, you or your doctor sends the bill to the insurance company. The company then pays you from the "pool."

 Pay your premiums on time. If you do not, you may lose your insurance.

Choosing a company

Agents. Choose an agent who:

- is experienced with newcomers to the U.S.
- takes the time to explain the different policies.
- does not try to sell you more than you need. You may want to ask a few agents how much to buy.

Reputation. Ask people you know about companies they use. Are they happy with the service? Were they satisfied with the way the company paid their claims?

Financial rating. If a company goes out of business, you may lose your coverage. Ask an insurance agent for the A.M. Best or Weiss rating to find out about the company's financial status. Try to use a company with the highest rating. Do not use a company with a rating lower than B (see "Chapter Information" in the Appendix).

Cost. You may get a discount if you buy more than one type of insurance from the same agent.

In general the amount of the premium depends on:

- the type of insurance.
- the policy maximum, or the most amount of money you are insured for. For example, a medical policy with a maximum of $50,000 for a single illness costs more than a policy with a maximum of $25,000.
- the amount of your deductible (see "Lowering the premium" below).
- the area you live in. For example, if you live in an area with little crime, your payments for home and car insurance probably will be lower.

Lowering the premium

Different prices. Compare prices for similar amounts of coverage.

Note: You may have more choice from an agent who sells insurance from several different companies.

Higher deductible. Your premium will be less if you pay a higher deductible; but you will pay more out-of-pocket money if you have a claim.

Discounts. You may get discounts for different types of insurance—for example if you have:

- safety devices in your home or car. Some safety devices are
  - burglar alarms.
  - extra fire extinguishers and smoke detectors in your home.
  - air bags that protect your body in case of an accident.

Your insurance company should have a license from the Department of Insurance for your state. Many state departments also have information you can get for free or for a low price. For example, the Department of Insurance in California has information about:

- the financial ratings of different companies.
- the cost for each type of insurance. This information helps you compare the costs of different companies.
- insurance costs for each region. This information helps you find out the difference between insurance costs for different areas.
- the number of complaints about the company.

Find the telephone number in the state government section of your phone book under "Insurance."

- – a club or boot that locks your steering wheel or tires.
- healthy personal habits. For example, you may pay less if you do not smoke.

Medical

Overview

Group plan. You and your family probably can get group insurance through an organization—such as:

- the company that employs you.
- your university (if you are a student or professor).
- a professional association (if you are a member).

A group plan is usually better because:

- it costs less.
- you will be able to get insurance more easily if you have a pre-existing condition.

Individual plans. Only a few insurance companies give individual coverage if you do not have a "green card" or a "pink card" or if you are not a U.S. citizen.

 Health insurance costs vary. An individual (non-group) plan may cost $100–$350 a month for one person or $350–$600 for a family with two children. Group plans cost much less. If you are an employee, your company will probably pay for part of the insurance.

The cost of health insurance depends on:

- the type of plan.
- the kind of coverage, or what it pays for.

- your gender (male or female).
- your age.
- your health.

What it pays for

Basic coverage. This coverage should include any care caused by the illness or accident—including:

- visits to the doctor.
- hospital visits.
- lab tests.
- surgery.

 Many companies have a ceiling, or maximum payment for a single accident or illness. Make sure this ceiling is high enough to pay your medical bills for this illness; if they are not, you will pay these bills yourself.

To get a "J" visa, the U.S. Information Agency (USIA) requires that you have a minimum benefit of $50,000 for a single accident or illness—that is, your insurance covers you for *$50,000 or more*. This minimum is a good guide for all newcomers to the U.S.

Other benefits. Some insurance plans help pay the costs for:

- regular check-ups.
- prescription drugs.
- maternity care.
- eyeglasses.

Dental insurance. With some plans, you may buy dental insurance as an extra part of your plan. Dental insurance may help pay for:

- routine care (cleanings, X-rays, fillings).
- emergency care.

- oral surgery.
- orthodontic care (for making the teeth straight).

Evacuation and repatriation of remains. If your permanent home is outside the U.S., you also need insurance for:

- emergency medical evacuation for your trip home—in case you get sick and cannot finish your stay here. The minimum should be $10,000, as required by the USIA for a "J" visa.
- "repatriation of your mortal remains," or returning your body to your home country—in case you die while you are here. The minimum benefit should be $7500, as required by the USIA for a "J" visa.

Limitations

Find out when the insurance policy does *not* pay. For example, ask if:

- you must wait a certain period before your insurance pays.
- the insurance pays for emergency care when you are out of town.
- the insurance pays for a pre-existing condition. For example, suppose you have had a heart attack in the past; make sure the insurance covers any expenses for another attack.

Types of plans

Indemnity.

With an indemnity plan, you choose your own doctor; the insurance plan pays for some of the expenses. The doctors are private; that is, they do not work for the insurance or health-care organization.

Two advantages are:

- You may choose any qualified doctor.
- You do not need to go to a primary-care doctor before you see a specialist.

Two disadvantages are:

- The indemnity plan usually costs more than managed care or an HMO (see below). Many sponsors and employers do not offer this plan.
- Probably, you will pay the doctor at the end of your visit. Then you must wait until the insurance company sends the money.

 In addition to the premium, you pay:

- a deductible of about $250 per person each year—or $1,000 for a family of four.
- co-insurance, or about 20% of the bill.

Most plans have a "cap," or a maximum amount you pay for medical expenses in a year; if the expenses you pay go above that amount, the insurance covers 100%.

Managed care and HMOs. With managed care and HMOs, you choose from a list of doctors or dentists who work with your plan. With managed care, these doctors are usually private; that is, they do not work for the insurance or health-care company. With an HMO, the doctors usually work for the health-care company.

Usually, you see a primary-care doctor first. To see a specialist, you get a referral from your primary-care physician. For example, if you have a "bad back," the primary-care physician may send you to an orthopedist, or bone doctor; if you go to the orthopedist without this referral, the insurance will not pay.

Ask:

- Who are the primary-care doctors and dentists on the list? Where are their offices? Does someone you know use and like these doctors? Do the doctors have the services you need?
- Who are the specialists? Will you be able to see a specialist who is not on the list? How much extra will you pay for this option?
- Which hospital will you use? Is it close by? Is it a good hospital?

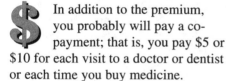 In addition to the premium, you probably will pay a co-payment; that is, you pay $5 or $10 for each visit to a doctor or dentist or each time you buy medicine.

The disadvantages are:

- You must use a doctor, dentist, or hospital that works with your plan. If you need a specialist, you may have little choice.
- You may not be able to see the same doctor or dentist when you visit; ask the company.
- The doctor or dentist may spend less time with you than a private doctor; ask other patients.

 My 13-year-old son brought home an insurance form from school. Do I need this extra

insurance? If you already have a family plan, you may not need any more insurance; but your child may need extra insurance if he regularly takes part in an activity that might cause injury—such as playing football. If you do not have medical insurance for the whole family, you may want to insure your son while he is at school.

My daughter is going to college. Do I need extra insurance for her? Your plan may still cover your child if:

- she is 18–23 years of age.
- a full-time student.

If your insurance plan does not cover her, you probably may buy:

- insurance through the college.
- extra insurance added on to your family plan.

Home and Property

Personal property insurance

This pays for your personal contents and extra living expenses if the property inside your home is damaged or destroyed. You may not need this insurance if you:

- do not have valuable items.
- are staying here a short time and have this insurance from home.

Before you get this insurance:

- make a list of valuable items— such as jewelry, furs, rugs, art, computers, and antique furniture.

- get a written appraisal, or value estimate, for each item.
- write down the serial numbers of cameras, computers, TVs, and stereos.
- give the list of your valuables, with the serial numbers, to your insurance agent.

Some policies pay for items that are lost, stolen, or damaged outside the home. For example, this type of policy pays if:

- you lose a diamond ring.
- you damage your computer while traveling.
- someone steals your wallet from a hotel room.

Liability insurance

If a visitor is injured in your home, you may be legally responsible. For example, you may be liable if:

- someone slips and falls on your front steps or inside your home.
- your dog bites your neighbor.

According to U.S. law, you may be responsible for the medical costs for these injuries—even if you are renting the home. Liability insurance pays for any legal and medical expenses you pay.

Homeowners insurance

If you own a home, you will also need insurance—in case your home is destroyed or damaged. Make sure the policy covers any special problems in your area—for example, earthquakes, floods, hurricanes, or tornadoes.

Auto

Overview

 You must have auto insurance if you own or rent the car you drive. If you own the car, your liability insurance must cover you and anyone else who drives your car regularly (see "Liability insurance" below).

If you are renting, you may buy insurance from the rental company (see chapter on "Getting Around"). Make sure you need this policy. If you own a car in the U.S., your auto insurance may also cover you when you rent a car.

Insurance may be expensive—especially for newcomers to the U.S. For example, liability insurance alone may be $700-$800 a year. Check with a few insurance agents to see how much coverage you should get. Also call the National

---

Be sure you understand the difference between the replacement value and the depreciated value. For example, suppose you paid $500 for a sofa five years ago. You might need $600 to replace that sofa, or to buy one like it. If your policy covers you for the replacement value, you get $600.

The depreciated value is probably lower, because the couch is older; this value may be around $200. If your insurance policy covers only the depreciated value, you get $200.

Automobile Consumer Hotline (see "Chapter Information" in the Appendix).

See "Cost" and "Lowering the premium" in "Overview" above. The cost for your car insurance also depends on:

- your driving record—for example, the number of car accidents you have had in the past.
- the type of car. You will pay more for a popular, expensive car. Check the insurance costs before buying a new car.
- the condition of the car. In general, you pay less for a car that is old or in poor condition; but you will get less money back if you have an accident. You may not want collision insurance for an older car.
- the age and gender of the driver(s). If you or a driver in your family is under 25, your cost will be much higher.

 If you have been here less than two years, you may not be able to prove that you are a safe driver; your insurance cost probably will be high. Sometimes, a letter from your insurance company at home will lower the premium; more often, it does not help.

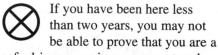 Every person who drives your car regularly must be insured.

Collision insurance

If two cars bump into each other, the collision insurance will pay:

- the damage to your car—if the car can be repaired.
- the value of your car if you need to buy a new one.

You may need to rent a car while your own is being fixed. Ask if the insurance pays for this cost.

Liability insurance

Suppose you are driving a car and your friend is in the seat next to you. If you bump into another car, you may be legally responsible for the cost of the:

- injuries to your friend.
- injuries to anyone hurt in the other car.
- damage to the other car.

By law, you must have liability insurance to cover the other person's costs. Each state has its own minimum—that is, the least amount of liability insurance you may have. In some states, the driver "at fault" pays all the costs; in states with "no-fault" systems, your insurer pays only for your injuries— even if you caused the accident.

 What if a friend drives my car and has an accident? Am I still insured? Yes.

Comprehensive insurance

This covers damage done to your car when no one is driving it—for example if:

- someone steals your car.
- a tree falls on your car.
- another car bumps into your car.

Life and Disability

 You may have trouble getting life or disability insurance if you are not a U.S. citizen or a permanent resident.

Life

Many Americans buy this insurance to protect family members in case the person who supports them dies. Some kinds of life insurance are also an investment, or a way of saving money. If an agent tries to sell you insurance as an investment, be careful. In most cases, other investments probably are better—if you do not need the insurance.

Disability

Disability insurance pays certain expenses if you cannot work for a long period of time. Your health insurance may pay your medical costs; you may need disability insurance to pay for your living expenses if you are not earning any money.

Words to Know

A.M. Best Rating: a rating that tells about the company's finances. An insurance company with a high rating (A or A-) will probably pay its claims and probably will not go out of business.

Ceiling: the highest amount insurance companies will pay for a medical service in one year

Check-ups: visits to make sure you are well. Usually, you go every year.

Claim: a right to collect money from an insurance company—for example, when you are injured

Co-insurance: the portion (%) of the medical bill that you pay after the deductible

Co-payment: a small amount of money that you pay for each doctor or hospital visit. Your insurance company or HMO pays the rest.

Collision insurance: insurance for damage to your car because of an accident

Comprehensive auto insurance: insurance that covers any damage to your car when no one is driving it—for example, damage from a falling tree

Coverage: the kind or amount of insurance you have

Deductible: an amount of money the insurance company *does not* pay. For example, with a $500 deductible, you pay the first $500 of the expenses; then the insurance company pays most of the rest.

Disability insurance: insurance you get if you are sick or injured and cannot work. This insurance helps to pay for your living expenses.

Evacuation: transportation to the nearest medical facility or to your home country

Financial rating: (see "A.M. Best" above)

Group plan: an insurance plan you get as part of a group

HMO: Health Maintenance Organization; a kind of managed-care medical insurance

Homeowners' policy: insurance you get when you own a home. The insurance covers damage to your home. It also covers liability and personal property insurance.

Indemnity medical insurance: a type of medical insurance. You may choose any doctor you like; the insurance company pays a specific amount toward the bill. Indemnity medical insurance is different from a simple payment, or indemnity, for an injury.

Individual plan: a plan you get by yourself—not as part of a group. You pay the full cost of your own medical insurance.

Insurance agent: a person who sells insurance

Liable: legally responsible for injury or property damage to someone else. You or your insurance company must pay the person you have harmed.

Liability insurance: insurance that pays if you have caused someone else or their property to be harmed. For example, you may be liable if someone falls and is hurt on your front steps.

Life insurance: insurance that pays if you die

Limitations: conditions that limit what the insurance company will do. For example, with a 6-month time limit, the insurance will not pay until six months have passed.

Managed care: a kind of medical insurance. With managed care, you choose a doctor from a list approved by the insurance company.

Personal property insurance: insurance that protects the contents of your home

Policy: a written agreement with an insurance company. You get a separate policy for each type of insurance—for example, health, home and property, and auto.

Policy maximum: the most amount of money you can get from the insurance company. For example, the maximum amount you may get from some medical insurance policies is $50,000—even if the medical costs are higher.

Pre-existing condition: an illness or injury for which you have been treated, medicated, or consulted with a physician before you bought the insurance. Some insurance companies will not pay for these illnesses or injuries—especially with an individual plan.

Premium: the yearly amount of money you pay for insurance on a monthly, quarterly, semi-annual, or annual basis.

Primary-care physician: a doctor who gives general care. With most managed care plans and HMOs, you must see a primary-care physician before you go to a specialist.

Quarterly: every 3 months

Repatriation: transportation to your home country because you are too sick or injured to continue working or studying here

Repatriation of mortal remains: transportation of your body to your home country

Semi-annually: twice a year

Serial number: the number stamped on items such as computers and televisions. If the item is stolen, the serial number may help the police find the item.

Medical Care

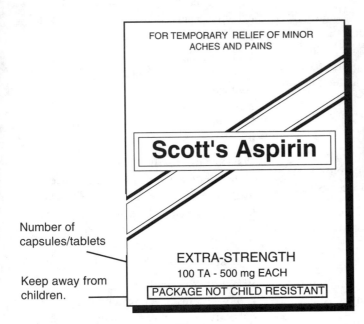

FOR TEMPORARY RELIEF OF MINOR
ACHES AND PAINS

Scott's Aspirin

EXTRA-STRENGTH
100 TA - 500 mg EACH

PACKAGE NOT CHILD RESISTANT

Number of
capsules/tablets

Keep away from
children.

Over the Counter

no doctor's order
needed

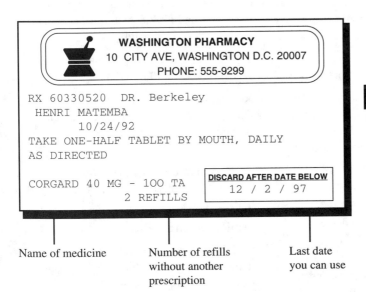

WASHINGTON PHARMACY
10 CITY AVE, WASHINGTON D.C. 20007
PHONE: 555-9299

RX 60330520   DR. Berkeley
 HENRI MATEMBA
        10/24/92
TAKE ONE-HALF TABLET BY MOUTH, DAILY
AS DIRECTED

CORGARD 40 MG - 100 TA
            2 REFILLS

DISCARD AFTER DATE BELOW
    12 / 2 / 97

Prescription

doctor's order needed

Name of medicine

Number of refills
without another
prescription

Last date
you can use

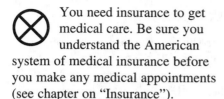 You need insurance to get medical care. Be sure you understand the American system of medical insurance before you make any medical appointments (see chapter on "Insurance").

Emergency Care

An emergency is a time when someone's health is in serious danger—for example, when someone:

- has broken a leg.
- may die from an accident or illness, or from swallowing pills.
- is unconscious, or can't be woken up.
- is burned by a serious fire.
- may be having a heart attack. Do not wait until you are sure; if you *think* someone *may* be having a heart attack, call "911" and ask for an ambulance.

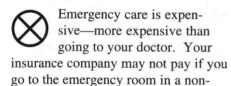 Emergency care is expensive—more expensive than going to your doctor. Your insurance company may not pay if you go to the emergency room in a non-

emergency situation. Find out when you can go to the emergency room and when you should go to a clinic or a doctor. If you plan to travel, ask where you should go for medical care if you get sick on your trip.

Your Visit to the Doctor

(see chapter on "Insurance-Medical" for different types of insurance).

 Visit the doctor soon after you arrive—even if you are healthy. Most doctors expect you to come for an "initial consultation." In some cities, the doctors are busy; many doctors are not taking new patients; be sure you have a doctor you like *before* you need one.

For your first visit to the doctor or dentist, you need cash, a check, or credit card to pay the bill; in some offices, you must pay for the visit and then collect the insurance later.

Getting to the hospital

Call **911** for an ambulance or go to the nearest hospital. Keep the name, number, and address of at least one hospital in a place where you can find it easily (see "Help!"—"In an Emergency" in the Appendix).

Non-emergency service

If you get sick in the middle of the night and you do not have a doctor, go to a nearby 24-hour clinic.

You will also need:

- medical records such as
  - medical history if you have a pre-existing condition.
  - immunization history.
  - dental X-rays.
- names or prescriptions of medicines you need.
- the name of your insurance company.
- your policy number.
- insurance forms for your doctor or dentist to sign.

Medicine

Choose a pharmacy that is close to your home or office. The pharmacy will keep records of your medications.

 Read the label on all medicine packages for instructions. Look for warnings—such as "Take with food" or "May cause drowsiness." If you have small children, look for "child-safety caps."

Overview

Over-the-counter or non-prescription drugs. These are for minor problems—such as common colds, headaches, and allergies. You can get these drugs at most pharmacies, supermarkets, groceries, and convenience stores.

Prescription drugs. Common prescription drugs are antibiotics, codeine, and birth control pills. You will need a prescription from your doctor. Some insurance plans pay for prescription drugs—but not over-the-counter drugs.

When you need medicine, call the doctor; have the number of your pharmacy ready in case the doctor wants to order the medicine on the phone. If your insurance pays for the medicine, bring your health insurance card to the pharmacy when you go.

 Ask your pharmacist or doctor if you may buy a generic drug (one that does not use the manufacturer's brand name); generic drugs cost 10%–75% less.

Abbreviations

ACU:	Acupuncture	**GYN:**	Gynecology
CD:	Cardiovascular diseases	**IM:**	Internal medicine
DR:	Doctor (may be a doctor or a dentist)	**MD:**	Medical doctor
		OBS:	Obstetrics
DDS:	Dentistry	**OBG:**	Obstetrics/gynecology
D:	Dermatology	**PED:**	Pediatrician
GP:	General practice	**RN:**	Registered Nurse (a nurse with a license to practice)
GER:	Geriatrics		

Eyeglasses/ Contacts

Who can help

Ophthalmologists are trained medical doctors. They mainly do eye surgery and treat eye diseases. Most also prescribe lenses for eyeglasses; a few fit you for contact lenses.

Optometrists are trained eye specialists. They mainly prescribe eyeglasses and contact lenses.

Optical shops

Many optometrists work in optical shops (eye centers). When you go to the shop, you can get an exam and pick out your eyeglass frames. Sometimes you may get the glasses in an hour; if you have a special type of lens, you may have to wait a week or more.

Most optical shops are open six days a week, from about 9 am– 6 or 7 pm. Often, you do not need an appointment. Call ahead for an appointment with an optometrist in a private office or for an ophthalmologist.

Alternative Medical Care

Overview. To find a trained practitioner of "alternative medicines," look for specific letters after the person's name. These letters show that the practitioner has completed a certain training or passed a certain test in the U.S. Some types of alternative medicines you may find are:

Acupuncture. Look for the following letters: Dipl.Ac. (Diplomate in Acupuncture); M.Ac (Master of Acupuncture); O.M.D./D.O.M. (Oriental Medical Doctor/Doctor of Oriental Medicine).

Chiropractic. Chiropractors heal many types of pain and illnesses; but they are particularly popular for back pain. The U.S. has about 45,000 chiropractors. Look for the letters D.C. (Doctor of Chiropractic).

Homeopathy. The U.S. has only about 3,000 accredited homeopathists. Look for the following initials: D.Ht (Diplomate in Homotherapeutics); C.C.H. (Certified in Classical Homeopathy); D.H.A.N.P. (Diplomate of the Homeopathic Academy of Naturopathic Physicians).

Massage. Call and ask what type of massage you will get. If the person on the phone will not tell you, do not go; many "massage parlors" provide illegal services. Look for the letters N.C.T.B. (granted by the National Certification Board for Therapeutic Massage & Bodywork).

Nutritional therapy. Every city has many "health food stores" where you can get minerals, vitamins, and natural foods. Also, most doctors often send patients to nutritionists for specific types of problems—for example, high blood pressure. Look for the letters R.D. (Registered Dietitian); D.T.R. (Dietetic Technician); C.N.C. (Certified Nutritional Consultant).

Osteopathic medicine. Osteopaths are particularly popular for lower back pain. Look for the letters D.O. (Doctor of Osteopathy).

Note: Many physicians practice alternative medicine. Physicians have the initials M.D. (Medical Doctor) after their name.

 Before you visit a practitioner of alternative medicine, make sure:

- your insurance covers this type of medicine.
- the person who practices the medicine is
  - accredited.
  - licensed to practice in your area.

Words to Know

Acupuncture: a Chinese way of healing using needles

Cardiology: the treatment and study of heart disease

Chiropractic: a type of alternative medicine that moves the vertebrae, or parts of the spine

Clinic: a place that treats sick or injured people. Some clinics are open all day and night.

Convenience store: a small store that sells different items—such as food, hot coffee, newspapers, and magazines. Many are open all night.

Dermatology: care of the skin

Emergency: a time when someone may die or may lose a part of their body—such as an arm or an eye

Filling: the silver that the dentist puts in any holes in your teeth

General practitioner: a doctor that handles common medical problems

Generic drug: a drug that does not use a manufacturer's brand name

Geriatrics: care of older people

Gynecologist: a doctor for women

Homeopathy: a type of alternative medicine that heals with very small amounts of certain herbs, minerals, or animal substances

Initial consultation: first visit to a doctor, or any other professional. Most doctors expect you to come in for an initial consultation *before* you get sick.

Internist: a doctor of internal medicine

Lab test: a test of your blood, urine, or other body fluids

Massage: a type of healing that uses rubbing, or touching

Maternity care: medical services for pregnant women

Nutritional therapy: a type of healing that uses diet, vitamins, and minerals

Obstetrician: a doctor for pregnant women

Ophthalmologist: a physician who specializes in eye care

Optometrist: a specialist in fitting and prescribing contact lenses and eyeglasses

Osteopathic medicine: a type of healing that moves muscles and bones to heal

Oral surgery: surgery of the mouth, teeth, gums, and jaw

Orthodontic care: dental services to straighten teeth

Out-of-area coverage: in a place far from home

Over-the-counter drug: medicine that you can get without a prescription

Pediatrician: a doctor for children

Pharmacy: a place that sells medicine

Prescription: a note from your doctor that allows you to get special medicine from a pharmacy

Refill: a prescription medicine that the pharmacy may fill again without permission from your doctor

Rx: a symbol for a medical prescription

X-ray: a photograph of the inside of your body

Credit Cards & Loans

Ms. Connally: Hello, I'm Beth Connally. How can I help you?

Mr. Tanaka: My name is Hiroshi Tanaka. I have a savings and checking account with this bank. I came to find out about getting a loan.

Ms. Connally: I see…Please sit down, Mr. Tanaka…What is the reason for the loan?

Mr. Tanaka: I want to buy a new car. The dealer will finance the car for me, but I want to see what terms this bank can offer.

Ms. Connally: I see…Let's talk this over…I'll need to know how much you are paying for the car…how much you want to put down…and how much you want to borrow… First, let me look up the account you have with us.

Note: Ms. Connally will ask Mr. Tanaka many questions about the loan and about his personal finances.

Credit History

What it is

Credit history is a record of the payments a person has made in the past and the amount of money that person still owes. This record is important for getting a credit card or loan and for doing many other kinds of business—for example, renting a home.

In the U.S., credit bureaus, or companies, keep individual records. Whenever you apply for a bank loan or a credit card, the lender or card company checks with the credit company or bureau. You will get the loan or card only if you have good credit history—that is, if your record shows that you pay your bills on time.

Unfortunately, the U.S. credit companies do not look at the payment records from other countries. According to the U.S. credit bureau, newcomers have no credit history. Without credit history, a card company or lender may not accept your application for a card or a loan.

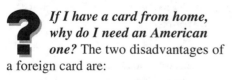 *If I have a card from home, why do I need an American one?* The two disadvantages of a foreign card are:

- The bill for a foreign card goes to your bank at home and is converted to the non-American currency—at a cost to you.
- You must keep a bank account in your home country to pay the bills.

How to get it

To get credit history:

- bring an American Express card from your home country (see "What to Bring" in "Before You Come" chapter).
- apply for a charge card at a department store you use (see "Kinds of Cards" below).
- apply for a credit card or loan (see "Getting a Credit Card" and "Getting a Loan" below).

You may need to "shop around"—that is, go to a few banks or stores. Bring a letter from your:

- employer giving your salary and position.
- bank at home (see "What to Bring" in "Before You Come" chapter). The letter should give your financial history.

If you borrow money or get a credit card, be sure to pay on time. After about six months, your payments will be reported to the credit bureaus, and you will have a good credit history. In fact, you probably will get ads in the mail from credit card companies asking you to apply!

 You may get a credit card from a credit union in 2-3 weeks. If you have a foreign American Express card, you may get a U.S. card in about 2 weeks. For any other card, you may wait 4–6 weeks for approval.

Kinds of Cards

Overview

Many Americans use credit cards to pay for bills over $10–$15. The two main advantages are:

- Paying with a card is simple and quick. Most merchants accept a major card with no questions asked.
- You do not need to carry a lot of cash in your pocket.

Many cards give bonuses—such as "frequent flyer" miles for an airline or hotel discounts (see "Getting a Credit Card" below). Most often, cards with these bonuses have higher interest rates.

With most cards you can get a cash from an ATM machine; this cash is good for emergencies or for extra expenses when you are traveling.

 Paying with a credit card is so easy that you may forget how much you are spending. Many Americans have stopped using cards because they had trouble paying their bills at the end of the month.

 If you have a card, find the "800" telephone number on the back; write it down on a piece of paper and keep it separate from the card. If you lose your card or if someone steals it, call this number right away—even at night or on the weekends. If you call, you may pay the first $50 charged on your card; the credit card company will be respon-

sible for any other charges made after your call.

What to get

Credit cards. You get a credit card from a bank. At the end of the month, you get one bill for all your purchases. On the bill you see the:

- total amount you owe. You do not pay interest if you send in a check for this amount within the set amount of time—usually about 10–15 days.
- the minimum amount you must pay for the month. This is not the whole bill. If you pay only the minimum, you will pay interest; usually, the interest rate is very high—much higher than the rate you would pay for a bank loan.

VISA and Mastercard credit cards are becoming more and more popular. You may use them in most stores, the post office, restaurants, gas stations, movies and theaters, travel offices, doctors' offices, and airports—almost everywhere you go.

Charge cards. You may get a charge card from a:

- company such as American Express or Diners Club. Use the charge card to get credit history (see "Credit History" above).
- store where you shop. If the store does not accept your application, ask for the manager at the Customer Service desk. Explain your problem; often, the manager may approve your application.

Charge cards from a store have some advantages:

- You get notice of special sales before anyone else.
- You may get a discount for opening up an account.
- If you cannot get a credit card, a charge card may help you establish credit history.

Debit cards. With a debit card, the bank takes the money out of your account right away. For example, if you buy $10 of gas with a debit card, the machine transfers $10 from your bank account and deposits it in the gas station's account. At the end of the month, you get a bank statement with the date and the amount of each sale.

Some banks offer VISA or Mastercard debit cards—rather than credit cards. These cards look just like credit cards; but the payment comes out of your bank account right away. Debit cards may be hard to get if you have no credit history.

 A debit card is like a check—only faster. Be sure you have enough money in your checking account to cover the payment. If you don't, the merchant will not let you pay with the card.

Getting a Credit Card

Where to apply

Your credit union or employer's preferred bank. If you belong to a credit union, your application probably will be approved. Most embassies and many businesses can get cards for their employees from a preferred bank.

Your university. Many banks give credit cards to students. Often, you can sign up at the orientation fair in September.

The bank or savings and loan (S&L) where you have an account. Ask about a credit card. If possible, bring a letter from your employer stating your position, salary, and income; but do not be surprised if you do not get the card.

The bank that has a correspondent relationship with your bank at home (see "What to Find Out" in chapter on "Before You Come.")

Banks that offer secured cards. A few banks give secured credit cards to people with no credit history. With a secured credit card, you deposit money in an account; then you can charge up to that amount with your card. If you cannot get a card in any of the other ways, this is probably the quickest way to get credit history.

What to look for

For help in choosing a bank that offers credit cards, call Bankcard Holders of America. (see "Chapter Information" in the Appendix).

Credit limit. The credit limit is the maximum amount you may spend in one month. For example, if your credit limit is $2,000, you may not spend more than $2,000 in one payment period. If you want to use your credit card for many different purchases, the credit limit is important.

Interest rates. If you will be borrowing money with your credit card, look for low interest rates. Ask about the interest rate for a cash advance (see "Kinds of Cards" above).

Bonuses. Many cards give bonuses—such as:

- frequent flyer miles on a specific airline.
- cash rebates, or money you get back for charging more than a specific amount.
- discounts for hotels, cruises, car rentals, long-distance calls, and other services.

Choose the card that has the airline or other bonus you use the most. If you choose a card with bonuses, remember these tips:

- Do not pay with cash if you can pay with a credit card.
- Pay the whole bill on time. Most bonus cards have high interest rates.
- Use a second card for credit. If you know you will paying for some things over time, get a second card with a lower interest rate.

Time. When must you pay the bill? The grace period is the time period between the date when the bill is mailed and due date—that is, the time when the payment is due. "No grace period" means you pay interest from the date when the bill is mailed.

Fees. You may pay:

- an annual fee for using the card. These may be as high as $50–$80. Often, cards with bonuses have the highest fees.
- a fee for late payments.
- fees for spending more than the credit limit.

Getting a Loan

Where to go

Loans may be even harder to get than credit cards. Again, the best place to get a loan is at a credit union, your employer's preferred bank, or a correspondent bank.

When you buy an expensive item, such as a car, the dealer may be able to get you a loan; compare the terms with those of other institutions.

You will wait 3–14 business days (1–3 weeks) for a loan approval.

 If you are thinking about borrowing from a finance company, be sure the company is reliable. Check the interest rates.

Kinds of loans

Installment loans. This loan is usually for expenses such as buying a car, paying for college, or fixing up your home; most often, you pay back the loan within 2–5 years.

Mortgage. This loan is for buying a home. Usually, you pay back the loan in 15–30 years.

What to look for

Down payment. The required amount is often 10%–30% of the loan; you can put down more if you want to.

Monthly payments. The monthly payment depends on:

- the interest rate.
- the amount of the loan, or principal.
- the time period of the loan.

Interest. Rates vary. Adjustable rates are usually less than fixed rates.

Time period. The time period is the number of months or years you have to pay back the loan.

Prepayment option. This option lets you pay back the loan ahead of time.

You will need a Social Security card or a W-8 form (certificate of foreign status). You may get a W-8 form at any bank. The W-8 form is for:

- diplomats or their family members.
- full-time employees of an international institution or their family members.
- teachers or students with a "J" visa.

These documents may also be useful:

- Financial reports. Bring a financial report from your home country (see "What to Bring" in chapter on "Before You Come"). Some lending institutions will consider this; others will not.

- Letter of recommendation. Get a letter from your employer stating
  - your salary.
  - your position.
  - the time you are expected to stay.
  - your visa type.
- Co-signature. If you need a co-signature, the lending institution will have a form for your co-signer or guarantor; the form states that the signer will pay your loan if you do not.

Words to Know

Charge card: a plastic card used to buy things. With a charge card, you pay one bill for all the charges you made in the month; you must pay the whole bill before the due date.

Correspondent (bank): having a special relationship with a bank from another country. For example, a bank in France may have a correspondent bank in the U.S.; if you are a customer of the French bank, you may be able to get faster and better service from the correspondent bank in the U.S.

Co-signature: a signature from someone else. The other person promises to pay if you cannot.

Credit: the amount of money that you deposit or pay into an account; the amount of money you can borrow

Credit card: a plastic card used to buy things. With a credit card, you get one bill for all the charges you made in the month; you may pay the whole amount right away—or just part of it, with interest.

Credit history: a record of your past payments. Your credit history tells whether you have paid your bills on time.

Credit limit: the maximum amount you can charge each month

Credit union: a type of banking institution. You can join only if you belong to a certain group, such as a group of employees.

Debit card: a card you use to pay your bills. With a debit card, the bank takes the money out of your account right away.

Deposit: to place money in an account; the money placed in an account

Down payment: a portion of the cost of a house that you pay when you buy a house; a deposit

Due date: the date when you owe the money. The bank or card company must receive your payment by that date.

Finance company: a company set up to lend money

Grace period: the time you have to pay your bill—that is, the time between the date when the bill was mailed and the date when your payment is due

Interest: money the bank pays you for keeping money in its account(s); money you pay for borrowing

Interest rate: a percentage paid for the use of money

Savings and loan (S&L): a banking institution

Buying or Leasing a Car

Minivan

Convertible

Cargo van

Sportscar

Sport/Utility vehicle

Sedan

____Parts of a Car____

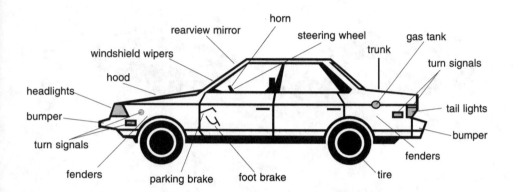

rearview mirror

horn

windshield wipers

steering wheel

gas tank

trunk

turn signals

hood

headlights

turn signals

bumper

tail lights

turn signals

bumper

fenders

fenders

parking brake

foot brake

tire

WORDS YOU MIGHT HEAR

2-door: a car with two front doors

4-door: a car with four doors. Two doors are in the front and two in the back

4-wheel drive: a car that stays on the road better because all four wheels have power. These cars are good for muddy roads and high hills.

ABS: a safety feature that keeps the brakes from "locking." It keeps the car from sliding when you stop suddenly.

Convertible: a car with a roof made of heavy cloth. The top can be folded back so you ride without a roof.

Hatchback: a car that has a door in the back. The door swings up, so you can put things in the open area behind the seat.

Sunroof: a window on the car's roof

Overview

You may:

- rent a car (see chapter on "Traveling In & Out of the U.S.").
- lease a car. A lease is long-term rental—usually 1-3 years. At the end of the leasing period, you give the car back to the owner; with some leasing contracts, you may buy the car at the end of the period.
- buy a car.

Getting the Best Price

The list price, or "sticker" price, is different for each car. In general, the list price varies with the make, model, size, and general features of the car.

New car prices

These prices depend on:

- the Manufacturer's Suggested Retail Price (MSRP); this is the price the company that makes the car suggests you pay.
- extras. You may pay more for extras such as air conditioning or a sunroof. Extras should be listed on the car window, along with the price for each.
- warranty. With a warranty, the dealer will fix any major problems for free or at a discount.

Used car prices

These prices also depend on:

- the person or business you buy it from. Cars sold by dealers usually cost more.
- warranties. Cars sold by dealers may come with a warranty; cars sold by individuals usually do not.
- the model year. Of course, a newer car costs more than an older one.
- mileage, or the number of miles the car has been driven. By law, the mileage must be on the

---

Find out about joining auto clubs such as the American Automobile Association (AAA). (See "Chapter Information" in the Appendix.) With the AAA, you get services such as:

- free maps and advice on highway routes in the U.S.
- towing. If your car gets stuck, AAA will come and tow it for you.

In some states, you may find the AAA under the name of the state—such as the California State Automobile Association (CSAA).

You may also buy a CD-ROM that maps out major routes between cities. Other CD-ROMs show how to get around each city.

odometer of every car—either used or new.

- condition. If you are buying a used car, have a mechanic inspect it (see below).

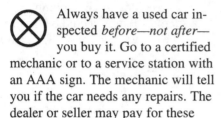 Always have a used car inspected *before—not after—* you buy it. Go to a certified mechanic or to a service station with an AAA sign. The mechanic will tell you if the car needs any repairs. The dealer or seller may pay for these repairs.

Other costs

In addition to the price of the car, you pay other costs, including:

- dealer preparation for getting the car ready to drive—such as cleaning and testing.
- insurance (see chapter on "Insurance").
- taxes. Taxes cost a percentage of the car price.
- title and registration fees (see "Registration" below).
- a car inspection fee (see "Inspection" below).

How long it takes

If the dealer has the car you want, you may be able to take it home right away—if you already have insurance. If the dealer has to order the car with special colors or features, you may wait six or more weeks.

Getting information

Before you negotiate the price, find out:

- the factory invoice price for new cars.
- the recommended price for used cars.

You may get these prices from:

- books and magazines at the library; ask the librarian at the "Information" desk.
- a consumer magazine—such as "Consumer Reports" (see "Chapter Information" in the Appendix).
- your credit union; many credit unions have books on car prices for their members.

How to buy a car

1. **Compare the prices at several auto dealers.**

When you enter the showroom, a dealer will ask if you need help. To look around by yourself, say, "I'm just looking, thank you."

2. **Ask questions.**

It is not impolite to ask a lot of questions and then say, "I want to look around some more" or "I want to think it over."

3. **Test drive the car.**

The dealer will let you take a short drive in the car.

4. Bargain for a good price if the dealer does not have a single-price policy.

Tell the dealer you know the factory invoice or the recommended price. Also tell the dealer what price you expect to pay.

5. Get a bill of sale *in writing* before you buy a car.

The bill of sale tells the price, the make and model of the car, and all the extras.

6. Discuss financing.

If you discuss financing with the dealer, also check out the terms with banks and other lenders.

7. Pay for the car or make a down payment.

You may pay with:

- a credit card. You may be able to pay with a credit card if you have one; but the dealer may charge about 3% extra—the amount dealers usually pay the credit card company.
- cash. Many dealers do not like cash.
- a check. Many dealers prefer a certified check.

Registration

 By law, you must get insurance for your car (see chapter on "Insurance").

If you buy the car from a dealer, the dealer will register the car and send away for the car title, or paper that shows you own the car. If you buy from an individual, go to the nearest Motor Vehicle Administration (MVA) or Department of Motor Vehicles (DMV) office.

 Call your state's MVA or DMV and ask what to bring. Most offices require:

- a photo ID.
- a bill of sale. For a new car, also bring the manufacturer's statement of origin; you will get this document from the dealer. For a used car, bring the title from the former owner.
- the name and number of your car insurance policy.

You will pay:

- taxes.
- a title fee.
- a tag or registration fee.
- a lien recording fee and contract, if your car is being financed.

Inspection

In most states you must have your car inspected for:

- safety—including lights, brakes, and signals.
- emissions, or the amount of pollution coming from your car.

The best time to go is Thursday or Friday afternoon. Try not to go during the last week of the month, when the stations are busy. Call the MVA or DMV and find out:

- where to go.
- how much it will cost.
- what to bring. Usually, you need
  - your car registration.
  - your safety inspection notice.
  - your emissions inspection notice.
  - cash.

Leasing a Car

Advantages

Easy return. You may give the car back when you do not want it any more. For example, if you buy a car and "trade it in," after a few years, you may still owe a lot of money; in fact, the price you get for the car may be lower than the amount of the loan you still have to pay.

Lower deposit. The down payment for a car loan may be 10%-20% of the price. With a leased car, the deposit is lower; sometimes, you pay no deposit at all.

Disadvantages

The total cost of leasing a car is often more than the cost of buying a new or used one. Add up the cost of the deposit and the monthly payments before you lease. Keep in mind:

- equity. When you return the car, you get no money for it. If you get an "open lease" (see "Your leasing agreement" below), you

may buy the car; but leasing a car and then buying it often costs more than buying it right away.

- penalties (see "Your leasing agreement" below). When you return the car, you may pay penalties, or fees, for
  - returning the car before the lease is over—for example, if you go back to your home country early; ask your employer if it will pay the penalty.
  - extra "wear and tear" on the car—for example, if the seats are dirty or the outside paint has scratches on it.
  - extra miles. You will pay a fee if you have used more than the number of miles in the agreement.

If you cannot afford to buy a new car, find out the price of a used one before you lease; used cars are often easy to sell. Often, leasing saves money only if you keep the car for a short time.

How to negotiate a leasing contract

1. **Get general information about leasing a car.**

Learn more about the advantages and disadvantages of leasing (see "Chapter Information" in the Appendix).

2. **Shop around.**

You can lease a car from:

- special leasing agencies.
- short-term rental car agencies.
- new car dealers.
- used car dealers.

3. Negotiate the price.

Do not tell the dealer you want to lease right away. Ask: How much does the car cost to buy? Negotiate. Then ask about leasing and negotiate again.

4. Compare the costs of leasing and buying.

Remember to compare the total cost (see "Disadvantages" and "Your agreement" above).

5. Read the contract carefully before you sign.

Your leasing agreement

How long is the lease? If you can, find out how long you will need the car. You will pay less if you lease for a long time.

How much will you pay? What is the deposit, or down payment? How much will you pay each month? What "extras" will you pay for?

What will you pay to break the lease?

Can you buy the car at the end? With a closed lease, you cannot buy the car at the end; with an open lease, you can. If you may want to buy the car, find out what the price will be.

What are the warranties? You should get the same manufacturers' warranties for leasing as for buying. Your dealer may ask if you want to pay for extra warranties; make sure you need these warranties before you buy them.

How much can you drive? With some agreements, you cannot drive more than a certain number of miles— for example, 15,000 miles a year. If you plan to drive the car much less, you should get a lower price. If you plan to drive more miles, find out if you will pay more.

Can you take the car to another city? If you plan to move to another city, make sure you can take the car with you.

What will you pay for "wear and tear"? The lease should say:

- what is normal "wear and tear" and what is excessive (too much). You will pay extra for any excessive "wear and "tear."
- how much you will pay for specific types of "wear and tear."

How will you pay for the tax? The tax can be as high as 10% of the price of the car. Who pays for the tax? If you pay, will the price be in your monthly payments?

What insurance do you get? How much money will you get if the car is in a serious accident? Will you get gap insurance—that is, enough money to pay the leasing company for the car?

Words to Know

American Automobile Association (AAA): a club for car drivers. It provides services—such as emergency repairs.

Bill of sale: a document that tells the price, make, and model of the car

Contract: a written, legal agreement between two people or businesses

Dealer preparation: what the dealer does to make the car ready

Deposit: (see "Down payment" above)

Down payment: the money you pay when you buy or lease the car. You borrow the rest (see chapter on "Credit Cards and Loans").

Emissions: gases that come from the back of a car

Financing: getting a car loan from a bank or dealer

Gap insurance: a type of car insurance. It pays for the difference between the amount you get from your insurance company and the money you owe the leasing company if the car is in an accident.

Inspection: a safety check on the car. All cars must pass inspection.

Lease: to rent a car for a long time. Often, you can buy the car in the end.

Lien contract: a document that shows the car is yours and who financed it

Lien recording fee: money that you pay the Motor Vehicle Administration to record that your car was financed

Make of a car: the company that makes the car—such as Ford or Chevrolet

Manufacturer's Suggested Retail Price (MSRP): the price the car maker suggests you pay. You may negotiate this price.

Mark-up: the amount of money the dealer adds to the price of the car after the car comes from the factory

Mileage: the number of miles the car has been driven

Model: the style of car—for example, Ford Taurus station wagon or Toyota Celica GT

Model year: the 12-month period when a new model is sold—usually starting in September

"No-claim letter": a letter from your car insurance company that shows you are a safe driver

Odometer: the meter that shows how many miles have been driven

Registration: listing your car with the state

Single-price policy: a policy that sets the price for a car. You cannot bargain to lower the price.

Sunroof: a window in the car's roof

Test drive: a chance to drive the car before you buy it

Title: a document that says who owns the car

Warranty: a guarantee that your car will work. If it doesn't, you can get it repaired for a discount or for free.

___Finding Work___

Ana Maria Castillo

222 Rockcreek Road, Arlington, VA 22052
703/999-2345

OBJECTIVE

To develop and implement training programs.

EDUCATION

M.A. Linguistics. University of Buenos Aires, Argentina, 1985.
B.A. Spanish Literature. University of Buenos Aires, Argentina, 1983.

WORK EXPERIENCE

9/95–5/96. U.S. Agency for International Development, American Embassy, Buenos Aires, Argentina. Training Coordinator.

- Developed a staff-development training program using resources from within the Mission and developing countries.
- Designed and executed workshops on subjects such as management and interpersonal communication.

8/90–6/95. The American School, Buenos Aires, Argentina.
Spanish Program Coordinator.

- Developed curricula for Argentinian and developing countries children in pre-kindergarten through 4th grade.
- Trained incoming Spanish teachers.

LANGUAGES

Native Spanish; fluent English; working knowledge of French.

REFERENCES AVAILABLE UPON REQUEST

Cover Letter

June 8, 1991

Dr. Steven Smith, Director
Training Services of America
123 Apple Street, NW
Washington DC 20000

Dear Dr. Smith:

I am writing in response to the advertisement in *The Washington Post* on Sunday, April 15, for the position of education specialist. Enclosed is my résumé and a newspaper article describing the Spanish program I developed for the American School in Argentina.

I believe I can contribute to the development of your language program for two reasons. First, my Master's degree in linguistics—with a specialty in Spanish dialects—is particularly suitable for the curriculum of your South American locations. Second, I have a proven track record; during the four years I was coordinator and staff trainer at the American School, student enrollment doubled.*

I look forward to speaking with you and will call next week.

Sincerely,

(signature)

Ana Maria Castillo
222 Rockcreek Road
Arlington, VA 22052

Enclosure

Note: The writer tells how why she will be successful at the job she wants.

Making It Legal

Who can work

If you are changing jobs or getting a new job, you may need to contact the Immigration and Naturalization Service (see "Chapter Information"—"Your Legal Status"—in the Appendix).

By law, you can take a job if an employer will sponsor you; but some jobs are more open to internationals. For example, professional jobs are much easier to get than jobs for secretaries, receptionists, or clerks. Also, people with technical expertise are in the most demand. Jobs in mathematics and engineering are easier to get than jobs in the arts, law, or medicine.

Professionals with jobs often can get work authorization for several years. If your employer is willing to be your sponsor, you may be able to become a permanent resident with a "green card" or a "pink card." Talk to an attorney if you plan to stay longer than the date on your visa or if you plan to change jobs—even within the same organization (see chapter on "Your Legal Status").

F-1 Students cannot work the first year. After the first year, you probably can work as long as you follow certain rules; check with the international students' office at your school. In general, you can work:

- on campus—up to 20 hours a week during the school year and full-time during vacations and holidays.
- off campus—up to 20 hours a week during the school year and full-time during vacations and holidays. The international students' office may help you find a company that has employed internationals before and is willing to do the paperwork.
- during vacation and after you graduate—for a total of 12 months; the work should be related to your studies.

Spouses. The rules for spouses vary—for example:

- spouses of diplomats. Some countries have agreements with the United States; that is, you can work in the U.S., and American diplomatic spouses can work in your country.
- spouses of international organization employees. Organizations such as the World Bank, International Monetary Fund, or the Organization of American States can sponsor you if you find a job.
- other spouses. The rules vary. For example, you may not work at certain types of jobs if you have a G-4 visa.

Getting Immigration and Naturalization Service (INS) approval can take 2–3 months or longer.

Documents you need

Legal documents. These depend on your type of visa. Ask your employer, the international students' office at your school, or an attorney.

Remember that some employers may be afraid of the law or of the amount of paperwork required. You might be able to get the job more easily if you tell an employer the steps to take.

Proof of qualifications. To prove that you are qualified, bring:

- translated diplomas/transcripts.
- training certificates from vocational-technical training programs.
- occupational licenses. Some professions need state licenses. To get the license, you need to take an exam. Contact the state licensing board.
- samples of your work—for example
  - samples of books or pamphlets you have written.
  - your portfolio if you are an artist or illustrator.
  - photographs or drawings of rooms you have designed if you are an interior designer.
- copies of any awards and honors you have received.

Looking for a Job

How to look

1. Complete the necessary legal forms.

2. Write your résumé and get samples of your work.

3. Get job counseling if necessary.

4. Look into job opportunities in your area (see "Job counseling services" below).

5. Call a possible employer.

You might say, "Hello, my name is Ana Maria Castillo. I am calling in response to the ad for a Spanish translator. Is the job still available? How can I apply?"

6. Send a cover letter and your résumé.

7. Go in for interviews.

Where to look

Want ads. Read the "Help Wanted" ads in:

- the classified section of the newspaper every Sunday.

- the "Professional Opportunities" listing in the business section of the newspaper.

Employers. Find out which companies may have the kinds of jobs you want. Look in the Yellow Pages and directories at the library. Many cities have books listing the most popular kinds of jobs and the companies that use professionals in those jobs. Ask each company if it:

- has the kind of job you want.
- is hiring or plans to hire soon.

If the answer is "yes," ask for an interview.

Networking. Talk to as many people as possible about your job interests and keep a list of possible contacts. Talk to friends, relatives, business associates, and neighbors.

Associations. If you join an association or professional organization, you will meet others in the same profession. Look in *The Encyclopedia of Associations* at the library for a list of associations. Call the main office of the association you want to join and ask for the number of the local branch for your city.

Most associations have:

- meetings about once a month.
- conventions with people from all over the country.
- training workshops where you can learn more about your field.

National Council for International Visitors (NCIV). The NCIV is a national program that helps international visitors meet Americans who work in the same profession. Call the national number in Washington DC to find out if your city has an NCIV organization (see chapter on "Making Friends").

International groups. You may get help in finding a job from an organization or center such as "The China Human Resources Group" or the "The Japan-America Society" (see "Organizations of Special Interest to Internationals" in "Chapter Information").

Many companies expect you to send your résumé:

- by fax. If you do not have a fax machine, use a private service—such as Mail Boxes, Etc.
- electronically. You may also need a different résumé for companies that scan electronically for certain key words.

If possible, get an E-Mail address and search for jobs on the Internet. Some career counselors estimate that more than one-half of the job openings are on the Internet. If you do not know to use the Internet, you may:

- ask a career counselor for help.
- look up an Internet service that explains what to do (see "Chapter Information" in the Appendix).

Note: Most libraries rent computers with access to the Internet.

Look in the business section of the White Pages; find all the organizations that start with the name of your country.

Job counseling services

Schools and colleges. Vocational schools, community colleges, and universities usually have a job counseling program, placement office, or career center. Also, talk to a counselor in the international students' office. Generally, colleges provide free job services to their students, including:

- self-assessment testing for help in planning your career.
- a career reference library with books that explain how to look for a job and what kinds of jobs you can get.
- job listings of government agencies and private companies who have job positions available.
- help in writing your résumé. Some career centers keep a copy of your résumé and send it to possible employers.
- on-campus recruitment programs. Employers visit the campus and talk to students.

The Continuing Education or Adult Education Department of many colleges also offers classes for people who want to find a job or start a career. These classes include:

- résumé writing.
- finding the best career for you.
- improving skills you need to get a job.

State and county employment service offices. Some services are free; others may cost up to $40 for one counseling session or up to $20 for a group session.

Private employment agencies. These agencies interview you and get you a job. There is usually no fee to you— just to the company that hires you.

Private counseling companies. These companies test your skills and help you decide which career is best. These programs may cost $1,000 or more.

Your résumé

Your résumé (see first page of this chapter) should include:

- your objective, or the kind of job you want.
- your name, address, and phone number.
- jobs you have had in the past. Include every relevant job you have had, how long you worked there, where the job was, and what you did (your duties). Try not to have time gaps, or holes, in

---

You can find books on specific careers, methods of finding a job, how to write a good résumé, and how to interview. Most bookstores also have books for the local area.

your résumé; make sure every year is included.

- your education. Include under-graduate and graduate degrees and special training classes that show you can do the job.
- special skills, such as languages you speak.
- names of publications or any articles or books you have writ-ten, even in another language.
- references. Ask first if the person will agree to be a reference. You may write references (names and telephone numbers) on the résumé, or simply write "Refer-ences available upon request."
- names of professional organiza-tions you belong to.

The Interview

Getting ready

Learn as much as you can about the job before the interview.

- Prepare questions to ask the interviewer. These questions
  - help you learn more about the job.
  - show the interviewer you are interested.
- Review your own skills and how they will help you do the job.
- Practice the interview. Find a professional or an American friend to help you prepare.

 Be on time! You may even be a few minutes early, but never be late!

 When you go to the inter-view, take with you:

- your résumé. Even if you have already sent your résumé to the interviewer, bring it along; the interviewer may have lost it.
- the names of references. Do not give these to the interviewer unless he or she asks for them.
- sample pages of your work. Give proof of your qualifications. Bring your portfolio if you have one.
- documents that show any prizes you have won or that tell about your work.

Getting a job is hard—especially for someone from another country. A professional career counselor will help you understand what to do and what to expect. For example, some counselors will interview you for prac-tice so you feel comfortable with American ways. Most professionals also look over your résumé and make suggestions. This help is important be-cause the American procedures and customs may be very different from those in your country.

How to interview

1. **Introduce yourself when you walk in. Shake the interviewer's hand.**

2. **Let the interviewer decide when to start talking about the job.**

Some interviewers like to start by talking about popular subjects—such as the weather, current events, sports, or international affairs. The interviewer will probably ask about your home country.

3. **Answer the interviewer's questions directly.**

Explain why you want the job and why you will be good at it.

4. **Ask questions.**

For example, for a job as a translator you might ask, "How long is a typical translation project?"

5. **Thank the interviewer for taking the time to see you.**

Ask when you may call to find out if you got the job.

May I ask questions about money? It is not impolite to ask what the pay will be; but do not negotiate at this time. Wait until the employer offers you the job.

Volunteer Work

If you cannot find a job, you may stay active by:

- taking adult education classes (see chapters on "Making Friends" and "Colleges and Universities").
- working as a volunteer.

To find information on volunteer jobs, check your local newspapers (see chapter on "Making Friends").

Words to Know

Association: a group of people who have the same interests or do the same kind of work

Career center: a place at a school that has information and people to show you how to look for a job

Cover letter: a letter that you send with your résumé to apply for a job. The letter introduces you and explains the details of your résumé.

Employment agency: a company that helps you find a job

Interview: a formal meeting between you and the person you want to work for

Local branch: a small office of an organization. The branch is in a different place from the main office.

Networking: meeting and talking to other people who do the same kind of work

Occupational license: a certificate from the government that says you are qualified to do a special job

Portfolio: examples of your drawings or photographs of your work

Recruitment programs: programs in which employers visit a school and interview people for jobs

Reference: a person who can recommend you for a job—usually someone who has been your manager or employer

Résumé: a CV; a document that describes your education, jobs, and qualifications (see first page of this chapter)

Self-assessment test: a test that helps you find out what jobs you can do well

Special interest group: a group of people with common interests—such as the environment or international relations

Transcript: a printed official copy of your educational record—the courses you took, and your grades

Vocational school: a school that gives training in practical skills—for example, carpentry or electrical work

Want ads: job advertisements in the classified section of the newspaper

Work authorization: official permission for you to work for pay

Workshop: an educational meeting—usually lasting a day or less

Your Children

Your Young Child

Day care International

3425 Franklin Avenue
Falls Church, VA 22134
(703) 437-8900

Child

Name Jung Kwon   **Nickname** John

Sex M **Birthday** 7/24/94 **Home Phone** 703/203-4124

Father's Name Ho Young **Work Phone** 202/627-8100

Mother's Name In-Ae **Work Phone** 703/436-2301

Emergency Information

Name of Child's Physician: Dr. David Miller
Phone: 703/371-5161

Name of contact persons if parents cannot be reached (2 names)

(1) **Name:** Peter Kwon   **Phone** 703-230-5117

(2) **Name:** Tae Sun Lee   **Phone** 703-230-8988

Persons authorized to pick up child:
Mother, Father, Peter Kwon, Tae Sun Lee

Persons not authorized to visit or pick up child:
none

Allergies: Chocolate, Bee Stings

Baby-sitters

Where to look

Other parents. Ask your child's day care or nursery school if you can post a note on the bulletin board. Often, other parents will share their baby-sitter with you.

Hospital and university nursing schools. Call the school's main office or the Dean's office.

Nearby universities. Ask for the career center or student job office.

Newspaper ads. Your local newspaper probably has ads for baby-sitters.

Baby-sitter agencies. These may cost more, but agencies can get good sitters right away. Look in the Yellow Pages under "Baby-sitters."

 First call the baby-sitters and get the names of three or more references. Call all the references and ask:

- How long did this baby-sitter work for you?
- Were you satisfied?
- What were the baby-sitter's strengths?
- What were the weaknesses?

Listen carefully. Do not be afraid to ask more questions. Ask the person to meet you and your child in your home.

Nannies/Au Pairs

Overview

Nannies. A nanny takes care of your child all day. Usually, a nanny is an experienced professionalwith special training. Some nannies live with the child's family ("live-ins"); others have their own home ("live-outs").

Au pairs. An au pair is usually a student from another country who comes to the U.S. for one year. Most au pairs live with the child's family.

Au pairs work about 45 hours per week. The hours may be flexible, depending on what you need.

How to find nannies/ au pairs

Agencies. Professional agencies will find you a nanny or au pair for a fee. Most check work experience, personal references, child-care experience, child-care training, or first-aid training. Some agencies also check criminal and medical records.

Nanny schools. You may get a list of graduates of nanny schools by calling the National Council of Nanny Schools (see "Chapter Information" in the Appendix).

Interviews and references. Nannies will come to your house for the inter-

---

When you leave, give the baby-sitter, nanny, or au pair:

- the name of the child's doctor.
- the name of your health insurance company and your policy number.
- the telephone number where someone call.

view. Agencies will check the nanny's references. Ask for at least three references if you have not gone through an agency (see "Baby-sitters" above).

 Make sure the person you hire has legal permission to work in the U.S. Ask to see a "green card" or "pink card" and a Social Security card. Remember: Hiring illegal aliens in the U.S. is a crime.

If you use an agency, you will pay placement fees. For example, you may pay a registration fee of about $50 to the agency to see the names on the agency's list. If you a hire a nanny from this list, you probably will pay the agency over $1,000.

Nanny. You pay the nanny a salary each week. You also pay some taxes for the nanny and possibly part of her health insurance. An agency will help you calculate these costs.

Au pair. When you hire an au pair, you pay:

- insurance fees.
- airfare to the U.S. and back.
- a weekly salary (usually less than the salary of a nanny).
- tuition for classes and spending money.

Schools/Centers

Day care centers. Most are all-day, all-year care. Children may go to most day care centers at any age. Look in the Yellow Pages under "Day Care," "Nurseries," or "Child Care."

Preschools, or nursery schools. Many have half-day programs; most preschools are closed during the summer. Often, preschools accept children who are:

- two years or older.
- ready for school. Children must be ready to leave home for a short while and play in the same room with others.
- toilet-trained.

Look in the Yellow Pages under "Schools—Preschools & Kindergarten," "Nurseries," or "Child Care."

What to look for

Go to the school or center without an appointment to see what it is like on an average day.

You may get information about day care centers and nursery schools from:

- educational counselors.
- guidebooks in local bookstores.
- the National Association for the Education of Young Children

---

You may send your child to a co-operative (co-op). Co-ops are centers and schools where parents help share the work in and out of the classroom. In most co-ops, parents help the teacher in the classroom— anywhere from once a week to once a month. Co-ops often cost less than other centers or schools.

(NAEYC). This organization publishes pamphlets that explain how to choose good care for your child. It also lists schools and centers that meet its high standards (see "Chapter Information" in the Appendix).

- people you know.

The staff's training.

- The director should have at least two years of college work in Early Childhood Education (ECE) and 1–5 years of experience in a child care center.
- The teachers should have some college training in early childhood education and a year's experience.

The staff's attitude. Do they like children? Does anyone on the staff speak your language?

The program. Some centers have many organized activities; others have more free play. For example, Montessori schools often have a lot of educational toys and games, with more free play than group activities. Each child is supposed to learn at his or her own pace.

Multilingual. Some schools have staff that speak two or more languages. To find the name and number of these schools, look in the Yellow Pages under "Schools."

 The Montessori philosophy is popular in the U.S. and in Europe; but any school can say it is "Montessori." To be sure a school really uses the Montessori methods, check the classroom yourself or call the Montessori Institute (see

"Chapter Information" in the Appendix).

The other children. Find out their:

- ages. Some centers have a wide range. Be sure there is enough care for each age group.
- backgrounds. Are there other children from different countries? Are foreign languages used by the staff?

Relationship with parents. Check to see if:

- you may visit anytime.
- there are parent-teacher conferences.
- the staff welcomes suggestions from parents.

Space and equipment. Look around the whole center, inside and outside. Be sure:

- the center is clean and cheerful.
- the equipment and toys are safe.
- the outdoor play area is a large fenced space.

Place. If the school or center is far away, make sure:

- the center will pick up your child for an extra fee.
- some of the parents live near you and will car pool.

Meals and snacks. Be sure the food is healthful. If your child cannot eat certain foods, find out what the center will give him or her instead.

Your child's reaction. See how your child likes the school when you visit.

Nursery schools

Calendar. Usually, the school year begins in September and ends in early June.

Each nursery school has different hours; but most run from 9 am–12 noon. Often, you may choose to send your child two days, three days, or five days a week. Some schools have full-day programs (7 am–6 pm) for working parents.

Class size. Usually, each class has about 14–15 students.

Who is accepted. All children must be ready for school—that is, ready to leave home for a short while and play with others in the room. Some nursery schools also:

- interview the child.
- give an Intelligence Quotient (IQ) test.
- require that the child speak or understand English.

Time: Many nursery schools and day care centers have a waiting list. Usually, they take the child who is first on the list. With some schools and centers, you may need to apply a year or more ahead of time.

Licensing. All good programs are licensed. To find out if a school is licensed, call the Department of Consumer Affairs for your city or county. Look up the number in the county or city government section of your telephone book under "Consumer Affairs."

 If you are already in the U.S., start looking for a nursery school about a year in advance—in September or October of the year before. Most day care centers accept children any time.

How to apply

1. **Call the school to make an appointment for a visit.**

Ask if you can bring your child.

2. **Visit the school.**

Talk to the director or principal. Take a look around.

3. **Fill out an application form.**

Send it to the school, along with the application fee.

4. **Put down the names of some references if necessary.**

Get the names of people who know you or your child. Call your references and ask if you may use their names.

5. **Have your doctor sign the school's health forms.**

6. **Take your child to the school for an IQ test if necessary.**

Most schools do not require this test.

Day care

Calendar. Day care centers operate either all year round or during the school year (from September to June).

Many day care centers are open five days a week; but some are open fewer days. Some centers, or "day-out" programs, let you leave your child for just one or two mornings a week. A few day care centers have "latchkey" programs; that is, you may leave your child for an hour or two almost any time you like. "Latchkey" programs cost more per hour than regular programs.

The full-time hours are usually 7 am–6:30 pm. Half-day programs are usually 9 am–1 pm.

Adult/child ratio. The National Association for the Education of Young Children recommends the following ratios for adults to children in day care centers:

- 0–12 months old. 1:4. Maximum group size: 8 children.
- 1–3 years old. Maximum group size: 14
  - 1:4 (under 2).
  - 1:7 (2–3 years).
- 3–5 years old. Maximum group size: 14–20
  - 1:7 (younger).
  - 1:10 (older).

Licensing. To find out if a center is licensed, call the Department of Consumer or Regulatory Affairs for your city or county. Look up the number in the city or county government section of your telephone book under "Consumer Affairs." If you can't read the name of the department, call "general information."

In some cities, the license is voluntary; some good schools may not apply for the license. In other cities, *all* good centers are licensed.

Special Needs

Most cities have services that test children for delays, or slow growth, in:

- speech/language, gross motor skills.
- audio/visual skills.
- psychological profiles.

Check for a program in the area where you live (see "Chapter Information"— "Your Older Child" in the Appendix).

Words to Know

Agency: an organization that will find a nanny or au pair for a fee

Application fee: money you pay to apply to a school

Audio/visual skills: (a child's) ability to see, hear, and speak well

Au pair: a person from another country who lives with your family and takes care of your child

Bulletin board: a board in a public place where you can put a message

Car pool: a group of people who go in the same car. Workers may "car pool" to the office or parents may "car pool" their children to school.

Cooperative (co-op): a day care center or school where parents share the work in the classroom

Day care center: a center where small children stay while their parents work

"Day out": a day care center where you leave your child for just a few mornings a week

Gross motor skills: a child's ability to make large movements—such as running, throwing a ball, or jumping

Illegal alien: a foreigner who does not have government permission to be in the U.S.

Intelligence Quotient (IQ) test: a test that measures how smart someone is

"Latchkey" program: a program that lets you leave your child for an hour or two—before or after school

License: a document that shows the center is approved by the government

Montessori (school): a school where children spend a lot of time playing

and exploring on their own

Nanny: a person who takes care of your child all day in your home

Nursery school: a school where very young children go, usually for a half day

Parent-teacher conference: a meeting between the parent and the teacher

Preschool: a school for children who are younger than five years old

Psychological profile: a test that shows how someone acts and feels

Reference: a person you call to find out someone's ability to do a job

Toilet-trained: able to use the toilet; not needing diapers anymore

Waiting list: a list of people who want to join a program or school

Your Older Child

Elementary School

Grades	Average Age
Kindergarten	5-6
Primary	
1st	6-7
2nd	7-8
3rd	8-9
Intermediate	
4th	9-10
5th	10-11

Middle School

Grades	Average Age
6th	11-12
7th	12-13
8th	13-14

Some systems have junior high schools (grades 7-8).

High School

Grades	Average Age
9th	14-15
10th	15-16
11th	16-17
12th	17-18

The School System

Overview

Usually, children go to school from the age of five or six and until the age of 18. At the end of the school year, most children go from one grade to the next.

The children get report cards 2–4 times during the year. The report cards tell if the child is passing—that is, doing well enough to go on to the next grade. You, the parent, must sign this card.

Calendar

Most schools begin in late August or early September and end in the middle of June. During the school year, the schools are closed for 1½–2 weeks in the winter—from the middle or end of December until around January 2. Schools are also closed for one week in the spring and on most national holidays.

Hours

School hours are different for each school. The day starts between 7:30–9 am and ends between 2–3:30 pm. Students—except those in half-day kindergarten—often eat lunch at school; in a few schools, children may go home to eat and come back again.

Public Schools

 The county or city manages the public schools. These schools are free for all students. They accept all children.

Finding a school

In general, children go to the public school in the neighborhood where they live. First find out which public school is best for your child. Then find a home in the neighborhood for that school. To find a good school, talk to:

- a relocation center or service.
- a real estate agent.
- an educational counselor (see "Tutors/Counselors" below).

Your child may be able to go to some special programs (see "Academic programs" below).

Academic programs

Levels of instruction. College-bound students must complete certain courses—such as a foreign language, algebra and geometry, and physics or biology.

Often, you can tell the level of instruction by looking at:

- College Admissions Tests such as
    - Scholastic Aptitude Test (SAT) or American College Testing (ACT) scores. Find out the school's scores from the guidance office.

- the percentage of students going to college and the colleges they attend.
- the kinds of courses offered. Most high schools have honors and Advanced Placement (AP) classes.

International Baccalaureate (IB). The IB program prepares students for the International Baccalaureate exam. Ask the school's guidance office if there is an IB program and how your child can get in.

Special-interest schools. Many cities and counties have schools for children with special interests or talents in subjects such as foreign languages, computers, math, science, or the arts. To find out about these programs, call the "Information" number in the phone book under your county's or city's public schools.

English as a Second Language (ESL) programs. In general, public schools have good ESL programs. Children from non-English-speaking countries take an English test before they start school so they can be enrolled in the right ESL program. Call to find out how to register.

Special needs. To find out about programs for the handicapped or learning disabled, talk to the principal or director of your child's school ahead of time.

If your child has trouble reading, writing, or paying attention, see if he or she can be tested for a disability. Ask:

- the principal or director.

- a private counselor.
- a learning center.

Note: Many local books about living in your city list the names of the good schools; look in the bookstore or go to Hello! America's website (http://www.hellousa.com/world).

Registering your child

Non-English records must be officially translated. Some schools will translate these records for free. Bring:

- medical records, or proof that your child has had all the required vaccinations (shots) and a physical exam. Often, the school can tell you where to go for free.
- school records from the your home country.
- birth certificate or passport.
- proof of residency (either a utility bill or copy of a document showing you rent or own a home in the area).

How to register

1. Call up the school's international students office or the "Information" number for your school system.

Make an appointment to register your child. Find out what documents you need.

2. **Have your child tested.**

When you go to the international students' office, your child may take a test in English and, sometimes, math. This test will help the teachers decide your child's program.

3. **Call up the school your child will attend.**

Ask about the orientation session so you can meet the principal and find out more about the school.

4. **Find out about open houses.**

Many schools have an "open house," or a day to meet with all parents.

Transportation

If you do not live near the school, the school bus may take your child. Ask for a bus schedule; find out if the school has "activity buses" for after-school programs or sports. The public school buses are often free.

Academic placement

Be sure your child is in the right academic class. For example, if your child had a different math program at home, he or she may be placed in remedial math classes—or classes for children having trouble understanding the work. Instead of a remedial class, the student might need a tutor (see "Tutors/Counselors" below).

The Parent-Teacher Association (PTA)

The Parent-Teacher Association helps you become part of the school. Any parent may come to the meetings and join the association. In general, a strong PTA means a better school. For example, the PTA may:

- raise money for school equipment or for field trips.
- talk about school matters with principals and teachers.
- hold meetings where parents get to know each other.

Join the PTA; volunteer your time if you want to meet people (see chapters on "Making Friends" and "Finding Work").

 What if my child is not doing well in school? Ask to talk to the teacher. If you keep trying and cannot get an appointment, speak to the principal. If you still have problems, you may want to talk to an educational counselor.

Private Schools

 Private schools may cost between $1,700 and $13,000 a year—with an extra $7,000 for boarding. Most have scholarships.

Kinds of schools

Bilingual schools. These schools teach in English and another language. Call your embassy or consulate to find a school with your language.

International schools. These schools have children from many different countries—including the U.S.

Religious schools. These schools teach religion along with other subjects.

Special schools. These schools have programs for children with special needs—such as children who are physically handicapped or learning disabled. Most of these schools also accept children without special needs.

How to look for a school

1. Find out if the school is accredited.

Also find out if the school is a member of a professional organization (see "Chapter Information" in the Appendix). To be a member, a school must pass a special review.

2. Visit the school.

Make an appointment with the admissions office; ask if you should bring your child. At the school, talk over the program with the head of the school or the admissions director.

3. Call the school's references.

The best references are people you know—co-workers, neighbors, or friends. You may also ask the director at your interview for names and telephone numbers of parents whose children attend the school.

 What if I need help finding the best school? Educational counselors can help. Many can give you advice about either private or public schools.

Applying for admission

If possible, contact schools a year in advance. You probably will need to send your application and school records by the end of February for enrollment the following school year.

When you apply to a private school, you will need an application fee and:

- a birth certificate/passport (sometimes required).
- translated school records.
- a health form signed by a doctor, which comes with the application.
- letters of recommendation from former teachers or people who know your child.
- an application fee.

What the school wants. Some schools accept only 10%–20% of the students who apply. Many parents apply to several schools at the same time.

Test scores. Some common tests are:

- the Secondary School Admissions Test (SSAT) for grades 5–11. Students take this test in local private schools and in test centers around the world (see "Chapter Information" in the Appendix).

- achievement tests for grades 10, 11, and 12. These test skills in subjects such as languages, math, history, and science.
- the Test of English as a Foreign Language (TOEFL). This test is given in many countries. Call the TOEFL office for times and places (see "Chapter Information" in the Appendix).

Writing samples in the child's own language.

Getting accepted

Most schools mail you a letter— usually by March or April. If your child is accepted, you probably will need to send part of the tuition at this time.

Tutors/ Counselors

If your child has special needs, call the Council for Exceptional Children (see "Chapter Information in the Appendix).

What they do

Private tutors and centers. Many tutors or centers teach several subjects. Some teach only reading and writing; others teach only math. Tutors may specialize in teaching English as a Second Language (ESL) or in preparing students for tests such as the SAT or SSAT.

Educational consultants. These consultants may:

- help you find the right school for your child.
- help you solve problems your child may be having in school.
- test your child to see
  - what he or she knows.
  - what his or her IQ (intellgence quotient) is.
  - whether he or she has some kind of learning disability.

What to look for

All tutors should be certified to teach in the state where they are teaching. Look for a special degree in one of these subjects:

- elementary education.
- the high school subject being taught, such as math or English.
- English as a Second Language.
- reading.
- special education (for children with learning or physical disabilities).

Fun Activities

School clubs

Schools offer clubs for outdoor activities and community services such as Boy Scouts and Girl Scouts; other popular clubs are science, drama, school newspaper, and international clubs such as the Model U.N.

City/county recreation

 If possible, sign up at least 2 or 3 months beforehand; the most popular classes fill up quickly.

Most county and city recreation departments offer programs for children of all ages—including sports, music, drama, and arts. Call the Recreation Department for the latest programs; to find the number, look under "Recreation" in the county or city government section of your phone book (see "Telephone Books" in chapter on "Telephone Services and Equipment").

 There is usually a one-time cost of about $20–$50, which includes any equipment and uniforms needed.

Words to Know

Academic placement: the right learning level for the point at which the child is learning

Accredited: approved by the government; meeting certain standards

Achievement tests: tests used by colleges and some private secondary schools for admitting students

Advanced placement (AP) classes: classes that let a student earn college credit while still in high school. You must pass a special test at the end of the course.

College-bound: going to college

Gifted and talented programs: challenging, or higher-level, programs

Grade: a letter (A, B, C, D, or E) that tells how good the student's work is; also, a school level—such as the first grade, second grade, etc. (see first page of this chapter)

International Baccalaureate (IB) diploma: a diploma that can be earned in addition to the regular high school diploma. Usually, the IB program is more challenging than most other high school programs. Many foreign colleges and universities accept an IB diploma.

Learning disabled (LD) students: students with special needs—for example, students who have trouble reading, writing, or paying attention

Magnet school: a school for students with special skills and interests

Parent-Teacher Association (PTA): a group for parents and teachers

Private school: a non-public school. Most students pay to attend.

Public school: a school that is paid for by taxpayers and run by the city or county. Public schools are free.

Report card: a record of a student's classes and grades

Tuition: the cost of an educational program. The tuition does not include other expenses—such as uniforms or books and materials.

Tutor: a teacher who helps an individual student learn a specific subject

For More Ways to Feel At Home . . .

Visit us on the Internet, where you will find:

❑ Personal contacts and advice about the area you will live in...especially for relocating individuals and families. Helps you choose the right home in the right neighborhood, schools for your child...

❑ Personal research and advice about college applications and programs...including financial aid. Helps you get admitted to the college that is best for you.

❑ Publications list—including books about living in U.S. cities, college admissions, American customs and communications.

Find out more!
Visit us on the Internet: http://www.hellousa.com/world

Higher Education

English as a
Second Language

What to Learn

 Basic English

 **Conversation**

 Reading and writing

 **Words for work**

 Test of English as a Foreign Language (TOEFL)

ac-cent (ak´sent) **Accent reduction**

How to Learn

 Classes

 Cassettes

 TV

 Phone

 Books

 CD-ROM

 Internet

How to Choose a Program

Program. What will you study? Ask:

- Do you want to learn English for everyday conversation and situations—or mostly for reading and writing?
- Is your goal to get a job or to study in a college?
- Does the school get you ready for the tests you need to take? For example, you need to take the Test of English as a Foreign Language (TOEFL) to study in most American colleges. You need the Test of English for International Communication (TOEIC) to get many business jobs.

Quality. How good is the program? First, make sure the school is accredited—that is, approved by a professional organization. Then find out:

- What do the other students think? Ask people you know who have studied in the U.S. Ask the school for the names of students from your country; call the students and find out what they think.
- Who are the teachers? Do they have degrees or certification for teaching English as a Second Language (ESL)? How long have they been teaching?
- Will you be learning at your own level? Does the school give tests to see where you should start?
- Will you get college credit for the program (see chapter on "Colleges and Universities")?

- How big are the classes? Does each teacher have 15 students—or 50?

Intensity. How much will you study? If you are coming to the U.S. for an intensive program, ask yourself how long you can stay. Also find out:

- How many hours of classes must you take?
- How many hours of homework will you have?

Location. Where is the school? If you already have a home in the U.S., find a school you can get to easily—either by bus, subway, or car. If you are coming for an intensive program, ask:

- Is the school in a big city or a small town? Which do you like?
- Is the weather cold or warm? How is it different from the weather in your home country?

Cost. How much does the school cost? In general, public schools do not cost as much as private schools. Ask:

- How much will you pay for each hour of class?
- Does the school have scholarships? Will you be able to apply for these scholarships?

Extra-curricular activities. Will you be able to find non-academic activities you are interested in? You may want to make friends and have fun at the school. Ask:

- Can you play the sports you like—such as tennis, basketball, or soccer?
- Are there classes or clubs for the arts—such as photography or painting, theater, or music?

- Is there a religious club you can join?

Services. Can the school give you personal help? You may want to get advice about careers and jobs in the U.S. If your program will be intensive, ask:

- Can the school help with immigration forms and rules?
- Will it help you find a place to live?
- Will it help you understand the tax rules (see chapter on "Paying Your Taxes")?
- Does it have a health insurance program?

Intensive Courses (F-1 Visas)

With intensive English programs, you study 20 hours or more per week. Often, these programs can help you get an F-1 visa. You can also take an intensive program if you come to the U.S. with another visa—for example, as a family member of a student or employee.

Applying

You can find out more about English-language schools from:

- American libraries overseas, such as the libraries at United States Information Service (USIS) offices.
- travel agents.
- the Internet. Many language schools are on the Web.
- the schools themselves. Call the U.S. Consulate or Embassy to find out if someone from the school will be visiting your country (see chapter on "Colleges and Universities").

Part-time Courses

Part-time courses have less than 20 hours a week of study. Most metropolitan areas have many classes to choose from.

Places to learn

Community Colleges. You may take ESL classes at a community college for:

- credit. Credit courses count toward a college degree. These courses are in a college's regular catalog. You usually need to be enrolled at the community college in order to take them.
- non-credit. These courses do not count toward a degree; but often

Many counties and cities have English language programs for newcomers. These programs cost *much* less than other programs. Often, the programs take place in the public schools; but they may take place in a community center or anywhere else in the community. Call the city or county and find out where it offers the class.

you get a certificate, which may help you get a job. These courses are listed in the "Continuing Education" or "Adult Education" catalog. You do not need to be accepted into the university to take them.

Courses at community colleges cost less for residents of the county or city than for non-residents. Usually, you are a resident if you have lived in the county or city for more than 6 months or a year. In some counties and cities, you are a resident only if you have paid taxes in that time period.

Public schools. Some public school systems offer ESL classes. Many large school systems even offer separate ESL classes for speakers of certain languages—such as Spanish, Korean, and Vietnamese. Call your local high school or look for information on these courses at the library. You will not get college credit for these courses.

Private language schools. Private schools and classes have many advantages. Usually you:

- have more choice about the time you go and the program you take.
- learn in smaller classes.
- get a contract at the beginning of the program. The contract sets learning goals, so you know
    - what you will learn.
    - how long it will take.

A few large schools have networks all over the world. With these schools, you can start learning English in your home country and then continue the same program after you get to the U.S.

Home study. You may learn from:

- books. Most large bookstores and some travel and foreign-language bookstores have books for learning English. Most major libraries have a variety of these books that teach English at different levels.
- audio cassettes. If you read English but want to improve your listening skills, try "books on tape." You can listen to these books at home or in the car. Also look for them at the library.
- videos. One interesting way to improve your English is to watch movies or operas in your own language and read the English subtitles.
- a course by phone from one of the private language schools. You will get books and sometimes other materials from the school. The teacher gives you the lessons by phone.
- courses on TV—usually cable-vision (see chapter on "News, Sports, and Entertainment"). Call the community colleges in your area and ask if they offer courses on TV.
- courses on the Internet.
- individual (private) lessons. Some private schools have instructors who come to the students' homes for an extra fee. Usually, the fee depends on how far your home is from the school. You will pay the cost of a private, or individual, lesson, plus the instructor's traveling time.
- CD-ROMs.

Advanced English programs

Vocabulary. You will learn idioms, common expressions, and the meaning of word parts.

Reading and writing. You will learn how to read more quickly, organize your writing, outline texts, punctuate and spell correctly.

Public speaking. You will learn to speak more clearly in formal or business situations—such as in business meetings or group presentations.

Skills for the workplace (also called English for Specific Purposes, or ESP). You will learn words used for a specific subject or job—such as law, business, computers, economics, or medicine. You may take these classes privately or in a group. Other schools teach work skills along with English—for example, accounting, typing, and word processing on the computer.

Accent reduction. These classes will help you sound more "American." Look for a program with:

- qualified teachers.
- a test to find out your accent level.
- small classes (no more than 5–10 students in a class).
- books, cassettes, or other materials to take home.
- 3 to 5 or more class hours a week.

Common Tests

TOEFL

You may have to take the TOEFL to get into a high school or college or to get a job that requires good English skills. The same schools that teach ESL usually have TOEFL courses. Test preparation companies also can help.

 The TOEFL is offered six times a year on Saturdays in August, October, November, January, March, and May.

Test centers. You may take the TOEFL at test centers in 170 countries across the world and in all states in the U.S. To get a free list of these centers, call the TOEFL office and ask for the TOEFL *Bulletin of Information* (see "Chapter Information"—"Colleges and Universities"— in the Appendix).

TOEFL classes help:

- beginners pass the test.
- advanced students write research papers, write business letters, and give speeches.

Test of English for International Communication (TOEIC)

Many businesses use the TOEIC to see how well you use English in everyday or business situations. Call International Communication Incorporated for more information on the schedule and cost (see "Chapter Information" in the Appendix).

Words to Know

Accent reduction: changing the way you speak so that others can more clearly understand what you say

Accredited: approved by a professional organization, such as the Teachers of English to Speakers of Other Languages (TESOL) (see "Chapter Information" in the Appendix). To be accredited, a school must meet certain standards set by the organization.

Certificate: a document that you get for finishing a class or course of study

Community college: a public, 2-year college that offers an Associate (A.A.) degree (see chapter on "Colleges and Universities")

Conversational English: a class where you practice speaking, not reading and writing

Credit: a unit of academic study in a degree program

English for Specific Purposes (ESP): a program for learning words used for a specific subject or job—such as law, business, computers, economics, or medicine

Intensive class: a class with more than 20 hours of study per week

Non-credit: courses that do not count toward a college degree

Private institution: an institution that gets its money from individuals and organizations, not the government

Public institution: an institution that gets a lot of money directly from the government. For example, community colleges get most of their money from the county government.

Resident (of a city or county): a person who has lived in the city or county for more than 6 months or a year—depending on the city or county. Some cities and counties also require that you have paid taxes during that time.

Scholarship: money you get to help pay for school

Subtitle: words at the bottom of a movie screen that are printed in a language other than that being spoken in the film

TOEFL (Test of English as a Foreign Language): a test of your listening, grammar, reading, vocabulary, and writing skills in English. The TOEFL is mainly used for applying to schools or colleges.

TOEIC (Test of English for International Communication): a test of your English skills in business or everyday situations. The TOEFL is more popular.

Colleges and Universities

AAR University

In the space below, evaluate a significant experience or achievement that has special meaning for you.

Last summer, I volunteered as a paramedic in the Peruvian partnership program. I chose this program because I thought it would help me decide if I wanted to be a doctor.

Those 6 weeks in Peru changed my life. At first, deep down, I felt that I was "above" the Peruvians I lived and worked with. Then, partway through the summer, I began to treasure their deep caring for me and for each other. I made friends with the neighborhood teenagers, who became closer to me than many of my friends back home. I began to admire my new family because they never argued with each other, even though they were very poor. And I envied the nurses in my clinic because they were so loving toward their patients, even though they knew so little about modern medicine.

When I came home again, my life seemed empty. So I began to choose my friends more carefully, picking out the ones who had the warmth I now longed for. I also started to choose activities that focused on my professional goals and on my desire to help others.

Now I am sure I want to be a doctor—the kind of doctor who makes a difference in her patients' lives. I know I will be a good doctor because I will learn everything I can about modern techniques. But I will also remember the lesson I learned in Peru: Modern techniques aren't enough. To be really good, you have to care.

Note: This essay is brief and to-the-point; it has no extra details. Second, the language is formal but not "fancy"; the student uses common, everyday words. Third, the essay is personal; it tells what the student thinks and how she feels.

Overview

Calendar

Colleges and universities offer courses for two semesters each academic year. The fall semester usually begins in early September and ends in December. The spring semester usually begins in January and ends in late May. Some courses are also offered during a shorter summer semester.

Each semester ends in a 1- to 2-week exam period. Vacations include 2–4 weeks in the winter and one week in the spring (see chapter on "Holidays" for a list of the national holidays). Some colleges have quarters (four sessions per year) or trimesters (three sessions per year).

Credit

Most colleges and universities use the credit system; that is, you get credit for every class you finish successfully. For example, you may get three or four credits for a class that meets for one hour, three times a week. To graduate from a 4-year, undergraduate college, you need 120 or more credits.

Transfers

Students often transfer credits from one college to another. For example, you may want to transfer credits:

- from an accredited college or university in your home country.
- from one U.S. college to another. Many students study 1–2 years in a college, then transfer to another college. Other students take 1–2 courses in another university—for example during the summer; then they transfer their credits.

⊗ If you are applying for admission to a college, ask the admissions counselor if you can transfer any college credits from your home country. If you are already a student here, ask your advisor if you can transfer before you take any courses.

Programs

Undergraduate programs.

- Associate of Arts—often called an Associate degree (A.A.). 2-year program used for credit toward a Bachelor degree or as training for certain jobs—such as

---

Read the "Chapter Information" section in the Appendix for places to get information about:

- applying to college.
- cultural activities.
- applying for a job.

the job of a secretary, technician, or physical therapist assistant. The most common types of college offering an associate degree are
- community colleges.
- junior colleges.
- Bachelor degree. 4-year program offered at most colleges and universities. In the U.S., this program is usually less specialized than in other countries. The most common programs are the
  - Bachelor of Arts (B.A.).
  - Bachelor of Science (B.S.).

You need a B.A. or a B.S. degree to get into most graduate programs.

Graduate programs.

- Master degree. 1-year to 3-year program for earning a specialized degree—for example, the Master of Arts (M.A.) or Master of Science (M.S.).
- Professional. Specialization in a professional field—for example the Juris Doctorate (J.D.) for practice of law.
- Doctorate. Highest degree offered by a university. Includes the Ph.D. (Doctor of Philosophy), the Ed.D. (Doctor of Education), and the Eng.D. (Doctor of Engineering).
- Post-doctorate. A non-degree program for people who already have a doctorate but want to research a specialized area related to their degree.

Non-credit programs. Most of these classes are open to anyone who wants to come. F-1 visa students may not take these classes as part of their program:

- audited courses. Academic classes you attend without getting a grade or credit toward a college degree. You do not take any tests or write papers.
- professional classes. Many 2-year and 4-year colleges have "adult education" programs for specific professions. Most of these classes are at night or on the weekend. Some programs give certificates to those who complete the class. Call a college or high school near you and ask for "Adult Education."
- enrichment programs. Courses for personal enjoyment or development (see chapter on "Making Friends").

Applying to College

 Submit your application materials on time—before the deadline. Most deadlines are in January for fall admission and in June

Most students do not study in the same university for undergraduate and graduate work. Even if you go to a college that is not well-known, you may be accepted into a "top" graduate school if you do well.

for admission in the spring of the next year. With some colleges, you may:

- apply electronically, or on the computer, if the mail will take too long.
- fax the application papers if the mail will take too long. Be sure you send the original application and other forms by mail afterwards.

Note: Some colleges have rolling admissions; that is, the college decides on each application about six weeks after it arrives. You will get a letter accepting or rejecting your application soon afterwards.

 When you apply to college, you need:

- an application. Often, this includes an essay (see first page of this chapter). Call or write to the admissions office; ask the office to send you an application. Be sure to say you are a foreign student.
- official transcripts. Allow plenty of time to order your transcripts from your home country. Send only original copies (no photocopies!) with notarized English translations. Get
  - college or university transcripts.
  - high school transcripts (for undergraduate admission).
- letters of recommendation from professors, advisors, or employers.
- medical and immunization records, with English translations.
- a statement of financial ability. To prove that you are able to pay

for your U.S. education, you may need to fill out a form. You may also need documents such as bank records and salary statements.
- admissions test scores (see below).

Getting information

Centers, libraries, and organizations. You may get general information about U.S. colleges for free or at a low cost (under $5). If you are in your home country, call the U.S. Embassy, the U.S. Consulate, or the Ministry of Education. Find out if your country has an advising center (see "Chapter Information" in the Appendix). Ask if there is a(n):

- Fulbright Commission or Foundation organization.
- binational center.
- exchange organization, such as the Institute of International Education or AMIDEAST.
- American university library.

Foreign Student Clearinghouse. This service may help you choose a college. You fill out a form that asks what you want—such as a major course of study and the size or location of the institution. Then the service sends a list of colleges you might like. Most Foreign Student Clearinghouses are in advising centers.

College guidebooks. All major bookstores in the U.S. have guidebooks with general information about choosing and applying to U.S. colleges. These books also have lists of most colleges, with details such as:

- majors, or academic programs.

- sports and other extracurricular activities.
- types of housing.
- costs.
- admissions tests you need to take.
- location.

For personal service to help you find the best college, visit the Hello! America website on the Internet (http://www.hellousa.com/world).

Materials from the colleges. You may get college catalogs and admissions forms from the colleges you are interested in; often, these items are free. Mail a letter or postcard to the admissions office of the school. Most catalogs have photos and details about:

- academic programs.
- requirements for getting admitted.
- academic calendar and application deadlines.

Many colleges also have videos and CD-ROMs detailing their offerings.

Academic and foreign-student advisors. You may talk to:

- the advisor or counselor at your high school or college.
- private advisors or organizations (see "Chapter Information" in the Appendix).
- the advisor for the community college you are interested in.

A counselor may help you:

- choose the right college.
- complete the forms.
- get help for the admissions test if you need it.
- find financial aid (see "Financial aid" below).

College representatives. College representatives often talk to students in their high schools or at college fairs. If you are still living in your home country, call the U.S. Embassy or the Ministry of Education to find out if any representatives are coming to your country.

College admissions counselors and students. When you visit a campus, you may have:

- a tour—usually with a student guide. With a tour, you walk around the campus and see the classrooms, dorms, sports facilities, and labs. Call ahead and ask when you can take a tour.
- an interview with an admissions counselor or student. The interview gives you the chance to talk over the program with a professional. With some colleges, the interview does not help you get admitted; with other colleges, you need to make a good impression with the interviewer. Call ahead of time and ask if you need to set a time for the interview; ask if the interview helps you get accepted to the school.

Most students apply to 2–10 colleges. Check with the admissions office or international students' office for each college you apply to. Ask how you can matriculate, or get admitted.

The admissions tests

The tests. The most common under-graduate tests are:

- Test of English as a Foreign Language (TOEFL).
- Test of Written English.
- American College Testing Pro-gram Assessment (ACT).
- Scholastic Assessment Test (SAT).
- SAT II (tests on subjects such as Math, English, World History, Biology, Chemistry, or a foreign language).

Common tests for graduate programs are:

- Graduate Management Admissions Test (GMAT) for business and management programs.
- Graduate Record Exam (GRE).
- Test of Spoken English (TSE), a 20-minute tape-recorded test of your English-speaking skills. Students applying for teaching and research assistantships often must take this test.

Preparing. You may prepare for any of these exams by:

- getting test-preparation books and cassette tapes from a library or bookstore.
- taking a test-preparation course
  - at a college.
  - at a private institute.
  - from a private tutor.

What to look for

Quality.

- Does the college have a good department for the subject you want to study?
- Is the college accredited? You may find this information in a college guidebook (see "Books to Read" in the Appendix) or from the college itself.
- Does the college have many resources and facilities—such as libraries, labs, research centers, athletic facilities, computer centers, and career counseling offices?

Cost.

- How much are tuition and other expenses (see "College Costs" below)?
- What scholarships or loans can this college offer you?
  Note: Most colleges offer scholarships only at the graduate level for international students.

Standards.

- What kinds of qualifications (both personal and academic) do you need to be admitted?
- Does the college admit a limited number of international students?

Requirements.

- Which courses do you need to take?
- How many credit hours do you need to complete?
- Will you be able to transfer any credits for college courses you took in your home country?

- Do you need to have a certain grade point average (GPA) to stay in the college?
- How much time do you have to finish the program?

Student body.

- Are the students from all over the U.S. or from one area of the country?
- How many international students study there?

Size.

- Is the college large or small? Which do you like better?
- How many students are in a class? What is the faculty/student ratio—that is, how many students are there for each teacher?

Location, extra-curricular activities, and services (see chapter on "English as a Second Language").

College Costs

Before you come to the U.S., you must prove that you can pay for your college tuition and living expenses. You probably will fill out a "Financial Certificate" that tells your "source of funds."

The college may estimate how much money you need for 9 months of study. Costs vary from college to college; private colleges generally cost more than public colleges.

Tuition. You may pay:

American colleges and universities may be public or private. Public institutions get most of their money from the local or state government. Usually, the tuition costs less than the tuition for a private college. All "community colleges" are public. Four-year colleges and universities with graduate programs may be public.

Private institutions do not get money directly from the government. Usually, the tuition at a private school costs more. Private institutions include both 2-year and 4-year colleges and universities.

Note: You get a tuition discount at a public institution if you are a resident of the city, county, or state. For example, a resident of Massachusetts pays less tuition at the University of Massachusetts than a non-resident; residents of Montgomery County, Maryland, pay less tuition than non-residents at Montgomery College.

Usually, you are a resident if you have lived in the city or county longer than 6–12 months before you enrolled. In some places, you must have paid taxes in the past year to be considered a resident. International students just coming to the U.S. are usually considered to be not residents.

- for each credit hour. For example, if a college charges $200 per credit, a 3-credit course will cost $600.
- a flat rate, or set amount, for full-time study—that is, more than 12 or 15 credit hours.

Financial aid

Scholarships, grants, and fellow-ships. You do not have to pay these back.

Assistantships. The college pays you to assist a professor with research, teaching, or administrative work.

Student employment. The college pays you to work for one of its departments or offices. Check with the Student Employment Office.

Loans. Ask the college or a private bank.

Senior citizen discounts (usually for people 60 years or older).

 Non-citizens cannot get a scholarship or loan that is paid for by the federal or state government. But you may get help from:

- the college itself.
- another organization in the U.S.—for example, an organization that gives scholarships to students doing research in a particular scientific field.
- an organization inside your own country.

Ask your guidance counselor, a private scholarship search company, an advising center, or your embassy.

Sample of 1996 Expenses for 12 Months*

Tuition and Fees	$ 6,930
Books and Supplies	$ 500
Food and Household Supplies	$ 3,500
Apartment Rental	$ 7,200
Clothing and Laundry	$ 700
Travel between School and Lodging	$ 850
Health Insurance	$ 375
Other Miscellaneous Costs	$ 1,750
Total:	**$21,805**

Note: If your spouse or unmarried minor child (under 18 years of age) will accompany you to the U.S. (F-2 status), add $2,975 per person to the estimate of expenses.

* This estimate is for the 1996–97 academic year at North Shore Community College near Boston.

Words to Know

Accredited: approved by the government or an independent agency; meeting certain standards

Admissions: applying to a school or college; doing all the necessary procedures to be admitted—such as filling out the application, having an interview, and taking the SAT

Advising centers: centers outside the U.S. with information about American colleges

Advisor: a special member of the faculty (college staff) who helps students plan their academic programs

Assistantship: financial aid for a graduate student

Associate degree (AA): a degree offered at 2-year colleges

Audit: to take a course without receiving a grade or credit

Bachelor's degree (BA or BS): a degree you get for finishing a 4-year program

College: a place for undergraduate study. Some colleges have graduate-level courses.

Community college: a public, 2-year college that gives an Associate degree (see chapter on "Learning English")

Credit hour: a unit of study earned by a student

Deadline: a specified date or time when you must complete or submit something; also called a "due date"

Degree: an award for finishing a college program—for example, a Bachelor of Arts or a Master of Science

Doctorate: the highest degree awarded by a university for advanced graduate research and study

Enrichment programs: non-degree, non-credit course programs on subjects such as art, literature, cooking, and sports

Extra-curricular activities: non-academic activities—such as sports teams or student clubs

Faculty: teacher

Fellowship: an award of financial aid, usually given to a graduate student on the basis of merit, need, and/or experience

Full-time: a student taking more than a set amount of credit hours per semester—usually, more than 12 or 15 hours

Grade point average (GPA): The average of grade points earned for all completed courses. Usually, A=4 points; B=3 points; C=2 points. For example, a student who has two As and one B has a GPA of 3.7 (4+4+3 divided by 3).

Grant: financial aid given to an undergraduate or graduate student—usually awarded to those who need the money the most

Higher education: post-secondary (after high school) education

Junior college: 2-year college. The college may be private or public—depending on the state.

Master's degree (M.A., M.B.A., M.S., etc.): the first graduate degree awarded after completion of a Bachelor of Arts or a Bachelor of Science. Usually, you study 1–3 years.

Major: a special subject area—such as psychology, economics, international business, or physics. Undergraduate students choose to take most of their courses, in this area.

Matriculate: to apply and enroll in a degree program

Private (institution): getting its money from individuals and organizations, or the government

Professional school: an institution for the study of business, medicine, law, or other professional areas

Public (institution): getting most of their money directly from the government. For example, community colleges get most of their money from county governments.

Resident (of a city or county): a person who has lived for more than 6 months or a year in a city or county. Some cities and counties also require that you have paid taxes during that time.

Rolling admissions: a type of admissions procedure. With rolling admissions, the college decides on each application within about 6 weeks of each application's arrival.

Scholarship: a kind of educational financial assistance awarded to an undergraduate or graduate student. You do not pay back the money.

Scholastic Assessment Test (SAT): the most common college-admissions test

Semester: a period of study lasting about 14-16 weeks. Many colleges have two semesters (fall and spring) and a short summer semester.

Test of English as a Foreign Language (TOEFL): the most common college admissions test given to foreign students

Test of Spoken English (TSE): a 20-minute tape-recorded test of your skills in speaking English. You might take this test if you are applying for a research or teaching assistantship.

Test of Written English (TWE): a 30-minute college admissions test that tests your skills in writing English

Transcript: an official copy of your school record showing the courses you took and the grades you got

Transfer: to get credit for college courses you have taken at another university

Tuition: the cost of a course

Two-year college: a college where you can get an Associate degree or certificate

Undergraduate: a person who is studying for an Associate or Bachelor degree. You need an undergraduate degree for admission to a graduate program.

University: a place for undergraduate and graduate study

For More Ways to Feel At Home . . .

Visit us on the Internet, where you will find:

❑ Personal contacts and advice about the area you will live in...especially for relocating individuals and families. Helps you choose the right home in the right neighborhood, schools for your child...

❑ Personal research and advice about college applications and programs...including financial aid. Helps you get admitted to the college that is best for you.

❑ Publications list—including books about living in U.S. cities, college admissions, American customs and communications.

Find out more!
Visit us on the Internet: http://www.hellousa.com/world

_____Staying Safe_____

Your pocketbook or wallet

- **Always** keep your wallet or pocketbook with you. Strap your pocketbook across your shoulder if you can.
- **Always** keep your pocketbook closed, with the locks facing you.
- **Always** keep your wallet inside your jacket pocket.

Your credit cards

- **Always** call the company right away if your card is lost or stolen.
- **Always** keep the number of your credit card at home.
- **Always** tear up the black carbon paper into little pieces.

Your money

- **Never** carry large amounts of cash. Carry a credit card or checks instead.
- **Never** count out large amounts of money where others can see you.

The Metro

Usually, the Metro is safe—even late at night. But:

- **Always** check the area outside the Metro before you go there at night.
- **Always** stand with other people in the station.
- **Always** stand away from the edge of the platform.
- **Never** pay attention to people who are arguing loudly; their partner may try to steal your wallet.

In your home

- **Always** make sure the area is safe at night before you buy or rent a home (see chapter on "Finding a New Home").
- **Always** lock your doors and windows. Most people have double locks, or locks that close two times.
- **Never** leave valuables near an open window.

Your children

Most people who kidnap children are not strangers—they are divorced or separated parents. But tell your children:

- **Always** dial 911 in an emergency.
- **Never** talk to or get into a car with strangers.
- **Never** let strangers into your home if they are alone.
- **Never** tell a stranger on the phone that they are alone. (Tell them to say you "cannot come to the phone.")

Your car

- **Always** keep the doors locked—when you are driving or leaving the car.
- **Always** put your luggage, tapes, and other valuables in the trunk *before* you reach the parking lot. (If you put your valuables in the trunk and walk away, someone may see you and get into the trunk.)
- **Always** carry a copy of your car registration papers in your wallet. Show these papers to the police if someone steals your car.
- **Always** have your key ready as you walk toward the car. Look inside quickly; then open the door and get in.
- **Never** leave the keys in the car.
- **Never** let strangers in the car.

At the bank machine

- **Always** be sure no one can grab you when you are using the machine.
- **Always** look around before you open the door or use the machine.

In a hotel

- **Always** keep your valuables in the hotel safe.
- **Never** leave valuables in the room when you are gone.

___In an Emergency___

Call 911

Fire

1. **Call:** 911

2. **Say:**

- "I would like to report a fire."
- "Please come to...
  (your address)."

3. **Tell:**
- which room the fire is in.
- how big the fire is.
- how the fire started.

Medical Emergency

1. **Call:** 911

2. **Say:**

- "I need an ambulance right away."
- "Please come to...
  (your address)."

3. **Answer questions** about the accident or sickness.

Crime

1. **Call:** 911.
Call if:

- you think someone is committing a crime—*do not wait* until a crime has happened.

2. **Say:**

- "I would like to report a (break-in, mugging, or other crime.)"
- "Please come to ...(your address)."

3. **Answer questions** about the crime.

Help will come in 5-10 minutes.

Chapter
Information

1. Before You Come

Telephone companies with International calling cards

AT&T: 305/938-5490; ask for the U.S. Direct Operator; call "collect" and AT&T will pay for the call.

MCI: ask for directory assistance for the number from your country

Sprint: ask for directory assistance for the number from your country

2. When You Arrive

Social Security Office: 1-800/772-1213. Telephone numbers and addresses of Social Security Offices near you.

3. The Telephone

(See "Chapter Information"—"Before You Come" and "Telephone Services and Equipment")

4. Your Legal Status

American Immigration Lawyers Association: 202/371-9377

Federal Information Center: 1-800/347-1997. Information on applying for local federal jobs, federal income taxes, immigration services, Social Security benefits—and other federal agencies, programs and services.

5. Traveling In & Out of the U.S.

AMTRAK: 1-800-USA-RAIL

Greyhound Bus Lines: 1-800/231-2222.

- North Carolina only: 1-800/342-6214.
- En Español: 1-800/531-5332

Hosteling International: 733 15th St., NW, Suite 840, Washington, DC 20005. 1-800/444-6111. Information on hostels here and abroad. For travelers of all ages.

11. Making Friends

(See "Organizations of Special Interest" below)

14. Your Mail

Western Union: 1-800/325-6000

16. Paying Your Taxes

Internal Revenue Service (IRS): 1-800/829-3676. Tax-related information. Publications:

- Publication 519, U.S. Tax Guide for Aliens

- Publication 901, U.S. Tax Treaties; Publication 513, Tax Information for Visitors to the U.S.
- Publication 520, Scholarships and Fellowships
- Publication 515, Withholding of Tax on Non-resident Aliens

17. Finding a New Home

National Association of Realtors: 202/383-1000

19. Telephone Services and Equipment

AT&T: 1-800/222-0300

Sprint: 1-800/877-4000

MCI: 1-800/444-3333

20. Insurance

Financial-status ratings of insurance companies

A.M. Best: A.M. Best Rd., Oldwick, NJ 08858. 900/420-0400

Weiss Research: 220 N. Florida Mango Rd., West Palm Beach, FL 33409. 1-800/289-9222

Tips on cutting insurance costs

National Automobile Insurance Consumer Helpline: 1-800/942-4242

21. Medical Care

Consumer Health: 1-800/DOCTORS (1-800/362-8677). Help in finding a doctor or dentist who speaks your language. All doctors and dentists have certified credentials that are approved by the organization. *Note:* Only doctors who pay are on this list.

National Health Information Center: 1-800/336-4797. Help in finding the organization that can answer special health questions on subjects such as: AIDS, cancer, alcoholism, diabetes, allergies.

22. Credit Cards and Loans

Bankcard Holders of America: 524 Branch Drive, Salem, VA 24153. 540/389-5445. Help in choosing a U.S. bank that offers credit cards. Publications: a list of banks that offer low interest rates and no annual fee. A nonprofit consumer credit education and advocacy organization.

23. Buying or Leasing a Car

American Telephone & Telegraph (AT&T) Automotive Services: 1-800/227-5327.

American Automobile Association (AAA): 1-800/763-6600

Consumer Reports Auto Price Service: 1-800/933-5555. Information about new cars, including the list price, the dealer cost of the car, and the price of options.

Federal Trade Commission, Publication Department. 202/326-3224. Publication: guide on leasing a car. 202/326-3175.

National Automobile Dealers Association: 8400 Westpark Dr., McLean, VA 22101-9985. 1-800/544-6232. Publica-

Organizations of Special Interest to International Residents, Visitors, and Job-Seekers*

The African American Institute: 833 United Nations Plaza, New York, NY 10017. 1-800/745-3899

AMIDEAST, Information Services: 1730 M St., NW, Suite 1100, Washington, DC 20036. 202/776-9600. Newsletter and information for students and trainees from the Middle East. The Mideast American Talent Clearinghouse (MATCH) links individuals currently completing advanced training in the U.S. and employers from the Mideast and North Africa.

The Asia Foundation: 465 California St., San Francisco, CA 94104. 415/982-4640

China Human Resources Group: 29 Airpark Rd., Princeton, NJ 08542. 609/683-4521. Recruits individuals for a broad range of management and technical positions with China-related businesses.

China Institute in America: 125 E. 65th St., New York, NY 10021. 212/744-8181. English and Chinese language exchange programs, field trips, films, lectures, and parties. For Chinese students, scholars, business professionals and families.

The College Board, Office of International Education, 1717 Massachusetts Ave., NW, Suite 402, Washington, DC 20036. 202/332-1480. Fax: 202/234-9806. E-Mail: jdeupree@collegeboard.org. List of Foreign Advising Centers. For foreign students applying toU.S. colleges.

Foreign Student Service Council: 2337 18th St., NW, Washington, DC 20009. 202/232-4979. Fax: 202/667-9350. Advice on college applications, financial aid, immigration, work and travel. Graduate-level International Leadership Workshops in the U.S. government and international trade and business. Special programs for Fulbright and other sponsored students. Publications: *Foreign Student Service Council Newsletter; Financial Aid Information.*

Independent Education Consultants Association: 1-800/808-IECA. Fax: 703/591-4860. Lists of consultants—including those who help with college admissions.

Institute of International Education (IIE): 809 United Nations Plaza, New York, NY 10017. 212/883-8200. Reference library with information about scholarships and studying in the U.S. Regional offices around the country; each region has its different services. Publication: Funding for U.S. Study, A Guide for International Students.

Japan-America Society: 1020 19th St. NW, Lower Lobby, #40, Washington, DC 20036. 202/833-2110. A variety of programs and services. Sends resumés to appropriate Japanese and American businesses and organizations.

National Council for International Visitors (NCIV): 1420 K St., NW, Suite 800, Washington, DC 20005. 1-800/523-8101. Fax: 202/289-4625. Provides local professional and cultural exchange programs for international visitors and scholars. Sponsored by the U.S. Information Agency (USIA) and the United States Agency for International Development (AID).

Partners for International Education & Training (PIET): 2000 M. St., NW, Suite 650, Washington, DC 20036. 202/429-0810. Fax: 202/429-8764. Places and monitors training programs in the U.S. for USAID-funded participants from developing countries. Does not provide funding for participants.

YMCA International Program Services: 71 W. 23rd St., New York, NY 10010. 212/727-8800. Fax: 212/727-8814. Variety of summer and training programs. Helps incoming students on international flights at major airports nationwide. Homestay tour programs for visiting students. Publications: *Group Educational Travel* (brochure).

* The list above is not complete. Look up the name of your country and review the organizations listed in the "Business" section of the White Pages or Yellow Pages.

tion: a "blue book" with used car prices.

24. Finding Work

America's Job Bank (www.ajb.dni.us/ cgibin/ajb/kickstart.fed). 250,000 nationwide listings.

Career Mosaic (www.career mosaic.com/cm). General-interest job bank.

Riley Guide (www.wpi.edu/~ mfriley/ jobguide.html). Explains how to use the Internet for finding a job.

(See "Organizations of Special Interest" below)

25. Your Young Child

North American Montessori Teachers Association (NAMI): 216/421-1905. (List of approved Montessori schools)

American Background Information Service. 1-800/669-2247. Background checks on nannies and au pairs

Child Care Aware Hot Line: 1-800/424-2246

National Council of Nanny Schools: 517/686-9417

26. Your Older Child

Private schools

The National Association of Independent Schools (NAIS): 1749 P St., NW, Washington, DC 20036. 202/462-3886 or 1-800/541-5908. Boarding schools and summer program directories

Montessori Institute, 2119 S St., NW, Washington, DC 20008. 202/387-8020

The Catholic Office of Education, P.O. Box 2960, Washington, DC 20017. 202/541-3135

Special needs

Council for Exceptional Children (a private organization for parents of handicapped and gifted children): 703/620-3660. Hot line resources

---

Admissions and English Language Tests

ACT test: ACT, P.O. Box 168, Iowa City, IA 52243. 319/337-1270

GRE: P.O. Box 6000, Princeton, NJ 08541-6000. 609/951-1100

LSAT: Law School Admissions Council: P.O. Box 2000, Newtown, PA 18940. 215/968-1001

Medical College Admissions Test (MCAT): P.O. Box 4056, Iowa City, IA 52243. 319/337-1357

Miller Analogies Test: Miller Analogies Test Coordinator, The Psychological Corporation, 555 Academic Court, San Antonio, TX 78204 (210/921-8801 or 1-800/622-3231)

SAT: Educational Testing Service, SAT. P.O. Box 6201, Princeton, NJ 08541-6201. 609/951-1100. Registration from abroad by fax: 609/683-1234

SSAT: Secondary School Admission Test Board, 12 Stockton St., Princeton, NJ 08540. 609/683-4440. Fax: 1-800/442-7728

TOEFL and TSE: Educational Testing Service, TOEFL, P.O. Box 6151, Princeton, NJ 08541-6151. 609/951-1100

TOEIC (Test of English as : International Communication Incorporated (LLC), 3301 Country Club Road, Suite 2205, Endwell, NY 13760. 607/748-9500

TESOL: Teachers of English to Speakers of Other Language, 1600 Cameron St., Suite 300, Alexandria, VA 22314-2751. 703/836-0774

TSE: (see "TOEFL and TSE" above)

across U.S., including *Help for Children* (a booklet with comprehensive list of hot lines and resources for gifted and handicapped): 1-800/343-0686

27. English as a Second Language

(See "Admissions and English Language Tests" below)

28. Colleges and Universities

(See "Admissions and English Language Tests" amd "Organizations of Special Interest" below)

Books to Read (Students)

English Language and Orientation Programs in the United States, Carl DeAngelis. Institute of International Education. 809 United Nations Plaza.

New York, New York 10017-3580. Over 1,000 programs and course offering of US acredited higher educational institutions, US private secondary schools, and US language schools.

Funding for U.S. Study. Institute of International Education. 809 United Nations Plaza, New York, NY 10017-3580. Describes 600 grants, scholarships, fellowships, and paid internships.

The International Student Handbook. By Allan Wernick. The American Immigration Law Foundation, 1400 Eye St. NW, Suite 1200 Washington, DC 20005. Attn: Publications Director

U.S. Taxation of International Students and Scholars—A Manual for Advisers and Administrators. By Bertrand M. Harding, Jr. and Norman Peterson. NAFSA: Association of International Educators. 1875 Connecticut Ave. NW, Suite 1000. Washington, DC 20009-5728

___Index___

Charts

Conversations

HELLO! T.M.
W🏛️SHINGT🌐N
a handbook on everyday living
for international residents

Award-winning

National Association of Directory Publishers Association
Best Page Design (1st prize)
Best Directory (honorable mention)

What Our Readers Are Saying about Hello!™ Washington...

"...a great job!"
Wendy Noble, librarian
Cushman, Darby & Cushman

"...a great source of information for international visitors planning to come to Washington...and for those who are already here..."
France Pruitt, President
International Education Associates

"...a wonderful book...answers so many of the questions I've been asked 5,000 times..."
Leslie Ivy, Manager, Human Resources,
Biotechnology Research Institute

"...wonderfully friendly and a practical source of information."
Jody Olsen, Executive Director,
CIES (Council for
International Exchange of Scholars)

..."saves so much time...You need to know so much, and this book has everything."
Marliene Casper
(foreign national, Germany)

"...a crucial primer for anyone just getting off the boat."
Kakhinder J.S. Vohra, New Delhi,
Managing Educator Association Trends

"...extremely helpful."
Raga Selim, Cultural Attaché,
Embassy of Egypt

"I recommend Hello! Washington to new immigrants and English as a Second Language teachers..."
Thomas Simon, librarian,
Prince George's County, MD

"Very impressive in every way."
Cmdt. Klaus Brommerschenkel,
Military Attaché, Embassy of Germany

"Wonderful book! I loved it!"
Marta Calderon,
Embassy of Costa Rica

"very comprehensive and practical."
David Austin, Vice President of Marketing,
U.S.-Japan Business Link, Inc.

"...simplifies all aspects of the adjustment process."
Nora Lee, Family &
Employee Liaison Office, CIA

"This book has everything you need to know before you get here."
Sandy Tsue,
Goddard Space Flight Center

"What a wonderful resource for all concierges!"
Sandy Brown,
Concierge, Classic Concierge

"...a wonderful introduction to U.S. life."
Gail Galloway, President,
Washington-Tokyo Women's Club